GAME
CHANGERS

FROM THE BOARDROOM TO THE BOOTROOM...

GAME
CHANGERS

INSIDE
ENGLISH
FOOTBALL

ALAN CURBISHLEY

HarperSport
An Imprint of HarperCollins*Publishers*

HarperSport
An imprint of HarperCollins*Publishers*
1 London Bridge Street
London SE1 9GF

www.harpercollins.co.uk

First published by HarperCollins*Publishers* 2016

1 3 5 7 9 10 8 6 4 2

© Alan Curbishley 2016

Alan Curbishley asserts the moral right to
be identified as the author of this work

A catalogue record of this book is
available from the British Library

ISBN 978-0-00-724764-6

Printed and bound in Great Britain by
Clays Ltd, St Ives plc

MIX
Paper from
responsible sources
FSC
www.fsc.org   FSC C007454

FSC™ is a non-profit international organisation established to promote
the responsible management of the world's forests. Products carrying the
FSC label are independently certified to assure consumers that they come
from forests that are managed to meet the social, economic and
ecological needs of present and future generations,
and other controlled sources.

Find out more about HarperCollins and the environment at
www.harpercollins.co.uk/green

To all football fans up and down the country who support their teams through thick and thin. I hope this book gives you an insight into the game we all love.

CONTENTS

Introduction   1

1 MANAGER   5
   Sir Alex Ferguson, Arsène Wenger,
   Harry Redknapp, Chris Powell

2 PLAYER   39
   Harry Kane, Mark Noble

3 LEGEND   61
   Rio Ferdinand, Steven Gerrard,
   Frank Lampard

4 RETIREMENT   107
   Jamie Carragher, Ryan Giggs

5 YOUTH   125
   Jón Thorsteinsson

6 ASSISTANT MANAGER/COACH   135
   Ray Lewington

CONTENTS

7   AGENT   147
Jonathan Barnett

8   CHIEF EXECUTIVE   157
Phil Alexander

9   BACKROOM   169
Wayne Diesel, Nick Davies, Steve Rigby,
Mark Maunders

10   FA   195
Greg Dyke

11   MEDIA   205
Jonathan Pearce, Nick Moody, Andy Cairns

12   INTERNATIONAL   223
Roy Hodgson, Chris Coleman

13   FAN   239
Ray Winstone

14   REFEREE   249
Mark Halsey

15   EXECUTIVE DIRECTOR OF FOOTBALL   261
Les Reed

CONTENTS

16 ASSOCIATIONS 277
Bobby Barnes, Richard Bevan

17 OWNER 297
David Sullivan

Acknowledgements 309

INTRODUCTION

I CAN'T REMEMBER exactly when I became hooked on football, but I'm sure like many other kids it happened at a very young age. In fact I don't recall a time when football wasn't part of my life. It just seems to have always been there.

I've been lucky enough to have been able to play the game professionally and continue in the sport as a coach and manager, but before all of that came along I was first and foremost a football fan. I still am. I was born and brought up close to Upton Park, and becoming a West Ham fan was never really in question for me or any of my mates. It was the club we all supported and the one we all hoped to be able to play for one day. I was fortunate to be considered good enough to train with them when I was a youngster, and privileged enough to be given match tickets to their home games. These were little green vouchers that allowed us to stand just behind where the dugouts were later positioned at the stadium. I would always try to make my way to the North Bank behind one of the goals and watch the matches from there. I remember some memorable matches looking on from those terraces, like the day Geoff Hurst scored six goals, including the first one, which he punched into the net, in an 8–0 win against Sunderland in 1968. I also watched on in despair as a great Manchester United side inflicted a 6–1 defeat on the Hammers in 1967, the season the visitors went on to win the league. So later on in my life being able to actually play for the club and manage – it was something special.

Having the good fortune to be professionally involved in the game for most of my life has given me an insight into the workings of football in this country, and during that time I have seen the game grow, change and evolve from those matches I watched as a youngster in the 1960s to the industry it now is. I wanted to go behind the headlines and the general media coverage to try to shed some light on exactly what happens in the game. To interview the sort of people who are part of the fabric of the modern game in this country, and who play, or have played, important roles in what football is now about.

There are some very familiar names included, but equally there are others who are not so well known, and perhaps some who are not known at all outside of the game. However, they all share something in common, and that's football. There are many people involved in the game and who earn their living from it. They are part of what modern football is about, and although it would have been impossible to include everyone who plays a part, I have tried to speak to people who I believe can shed some light on the workings of the game at the top in this country.

Supporters see their favourite team or player running out onto the field each week, but might not have any idea about those involved in making sure that can happen – people such as the coaches, the medical and sports science team, the player liaison officers and the kit men. They all play their part, and that is why I have tried to talk to a broad cross-section of people from the boardroom to the bootroom.

Things are always changing in football, with managers, players and others involved in the game moving on or changing clubs. The vast majority of the interviews I conducted took place in 2015, with the others happening in the early part of 2016. Although circumstances may have changed for some of the people I spoke to at the time, I hope the relevance of what they told me and the candid way in which they were prepared to speak about their roles within the game give the sort of insight that fans will be interested in.

Football at the highest level might now be an industry, but at the same time it is still a very simple game with very simple rules. The drama, spectacle, excitement, happiness and sadness that come along with it make it special for those of us who love it. Once you're hooked, football becomes an addiction – and it stays with you for life.

CHAPTER 1

MANAGER

Sir Alex Ferguson, Arsène Wenger,
Harry Redknapp, Chris Powell

WHEN IT COMES to talking about football management in Britain there is probably only one place to start. If you've won two Champions League finals, a couple of European Cup Winners' Cups, seventeen domestic league titles and fourteen domestic cup competitions, the chances are you know what you've been doing. Add to all of that a managerial career that lasted for almost forty years, twenty-seven of which were spent at Manchester United – one of the biggest clubs in the world – and you can see why Sir Alex Ferguson has rightly earned legendary status as one of the greatest managers of all time.

He took his first steps in management in 1974 with East Stirlingshire in Scotland, and then went on to have success with St Mirren, winning the Scottish First Division, before taking over at Aberdeen for eight years, during which time he won three Scottish Premier Division titles, four Scottish Cups, one League Cup and, perhaps most remarkably of all, the European Cup Winners' Cup. During his spell at United he not only won the Champions League twice, he also guided his teams to an incredible thirteen Premier League titles in the space of twenty years. He built and rebuilt his United teams, producing an attacking brand of football that enabled the club to become consistent winners.

Throughout his time as a manager his fierce drive and determination to win stayed at the centre of what he was about, producing teams on either side of the border that were successful and entertaining. As a manager I faced Alex's teams on several occasions, and the one thing you could always be sure of was that they were going to come after you and attack, whether it was at Old Trafford or your own ground. His teams played in a certain way and were incredibly successful as a result.

'It was the way I was,' he says. 'At Aberdeen I always played with two wide players and at St Mirren I always played with two wide players, and I always had a player who'd play off the centre-forward. When I started as a player I had a wee bit of pace, but when I got towards the end of my career I used to drop in and it's a problem for defenders. Brian McClair was the first one to do it for me at United, when I had Mark Hughes with him. Then it was Hughes and Cantona, then it was Andy Cole and Cantona. I've always done it.'

Something else he always did as a manager was to go for

a win where others might have settled for a draw. I remember some years ago Alex telling me he didn't do draws, and he'd often end up with five forwards on the pitch because he always wanted those three points.

'Yes, that's why I was prepared to take a risk in the last fifteen minutes of a game,' he admits. 'We just threw them all up front! Sometimes it was dictated by substitutions our opponents made. A lot of them would put a defender on, that gave me the licence to bring an extra forward on. Reducing their own attacking position meant I could risk it. I think risk is part of football. I never worried about it. I was always happy to have a gamble.'

Those gambles paid off on so many occasions for United, and they were something that ran right through his time at the club. Players came and players went, teams were built and then rebuilt, but the level of success never dropped as United consistently won trophies. Yet it wasn't all about success for Alex during his early years at the club, and after three years with them he hit what was to be one of his worst periods in management.

'I had a really bad period at United in 1989,' he recalls. 'In the whole of December I never won a game. We had a lot of injuries. But no matter who you are your job is to win games, and it was probably a lesson for me in how to handle that part of the game. At United you're expected to win. That's the expectation – and it was a great lesson for me. I used to pick teams with five players injured, and the games in December come one on top of the other during that Christmas and New Year period.

'I remember we played Crystal Palace at home and lost 2–1, and we were 1–0 up. It was one of those horrible rainy days in Manchester, and when I got home I got a call to say we'd drawn Nottingham Forest away in the FA Cup, who at that time were arguably the best cup team in the country. When we got to that game we still had a lot of players injured. You'd find it impossible to think that the team won that day, but they did. We had players playing out of position, we had Ince out, Danny Wallace out, Neil Webb was out – and we won. We won 1–0 when Mark Robins scored. One of the best crossers I had at United, of all time, was not a winger. It was Mark Hughes. He was a fantastic crosser of a ball, with either foot. He got the ball on the wing and then bent it in with the outside of his foot. In actual fact, Stuart Pearce shoved Mark Robins on to the ball and he scored. We won, went through and won the cup that season.'

The FA Cup win in 1990 after a replay against Crystal Palace at Wembley was the first trophy Alex won as United manager, and it was followed the next season by victory in the European Cup Winners' Cup. In 1993 United became the first winners of the newly formed Premier League. That year not only ushered in a golden period for United in terms of their title-winning ability as a club. It was also the dawn of a new era in English football, with television money playing a significantly more prominent role for those clubs who were part of the Premier League. It was one of the major changes to take place during the time he was in charge, although there have been others that he feels have had an impact on managers.

'I came into management before Sky really took off. I started in 1974 when I was thirty-two years of age, so when those various changes happened and the explosion came I had the experience to handle all of that,' he says. 'You integrated into all the various changes, so in terms of dealing with players at that time I could see if there was a change in the player's personality because of the success we were having. I could deal with that because I had a few years behind me. I always remember when I started at Aberdeen the vice-chairman, Chris Anderson, said to me, "We need to be at the top of the Scottish Premier Division when satellite television comes in." I had absolutely no idea what he meant, but I didn't want to say, "What do you mean?" It just registered in my head that I had to be successful. The way Sky have elevated the game and made all these players film stars, in terms of the way they are recognised now – that changed everything. But the one place you wanted to be was the Premier League.

'The other thing which changed was ownership of clubs. You wonder why these owners – from America, from China, from the Middle East – why are they there? Is it because of television? I think it must be part of the reason. Can you imagine if Premier League teams were allowed to sell their own television rights? It's never happened, but you say to yourself, "Well, it may change." If Manchester United were to sell their television rights they'd be comfortably the biggest club in the world.

'The other change of course was the Bosman rule. It was a massive change and it caught us all on the hop. Nobody expected it. All of a sudden you were panicking, and that created the explosion of agents – there's no doubt about that. You had guys who were agents in the music industry who wanted to be football agents, and that was a seismic change for managers, having to deal with all that. So the manager had the training through the week, he's got to pick the team on the Saturday, he's got a board meeting to answer to directors and he's got his television interviews. But on top of that you've got agents plugging away. They're maybe phoning other clubs – "My player's not happy" – we know it happens, not everyone, but some of them do, and they negotiate with you knowing they've got a full deck of cards under the table. "Well, we'll think about it." I don't know how many times I've heard that – "We'll think about your offer."

'If you were to write down the things a manager has to deal with, managers wouldn't want to be managing! They have a massive task – the managers of today – massive, and the media is a big problem. They are under pressure. They need to be successful – just like managers – and get a piece in the papers, but they're up against things like the internet and Sky television. They used to run my press conference on a Friday, or bits of it, through the whole day. That used to get me really annoyed.'

Alex has always had a great affinity with other managers, and was invariably there to wish a young manager luck when they got their first job. He knows just what a tough profession it is for everyone, whether they achieve the level of success he has had with a top club like Manchester United or simply toil away in the lower leagues. They are at either end of the managerial spectrum, and then there are all the other managers in between who do a great job week in and week out but perhaps never hit the headlines. Only a handful of managers can win trophies or get their side promoted each season, but so many others have done fantastically well throughout their careers, and it's clear he not only values them as friends but also knows just what good work they've done.

'When I was at Aberdeen the most regular calls I used to get about players in Scotland were from Lennie Lawrence, who was at Charlton, and John Rudge, who was at Port Vale. Rudgie must have been on the lowest budget in the history of the game! But he used to live with that. He would find a way of getting players on loan, and only if you've been in the job do you realise how difficult that is. Lennie Lawrence would be on the phone asking about players, and when I first came down to England, if you went to a reserve game these same guys were at the matches.

'They were a great example of perseverance and staying in the game – surviving. They were good guys and I enjoyed working with them. David Pleat was another one who phoned a lot, and Mel Machin, who was at Norwich. When I came down to England I relied on one person for my information on other teams – John Lyall at West Ham. John Lyall and I met on holiday once and we got very friendly. When I came down here he was fantastic for me. He sent me all his reports on the players, the games, the teams. For the nine months until I got my feet under the table, got my scouting staff sorted out, he was very good to me.

'There were quite a few managers I knew reasonably well, like Keith Burkinshaw, and another manager who needs recognition is Dario Gradi, who was at Crewe – and he's still there. You look at these managers, the Lawrences and the Rudges, they're still in the game. So they were there before I came and they were there after I've left! Realistically, you should have a reasonable amount of success with a club like Manchester United. With the resources, the history – you should have reasonable success. These guys have a place in the game. They've not won the FA Cup, or the Premier League or European cups, and they've had harder jobs than I've had. If you look at Lennie Lawrence and John Rudge, their success has been relative to their resources. As a manager it's up to you to make the best of what you've got.'

You don't stay in any job for as long as Alex did without being able to adapt and change as the game around you changes. I think his ability to do this, and at the same time retain the kind of football beliefs and attitude he always had, was a key factor for him. He embraced change and innovation but at the same time trusted his own ability and experience as a manager, maintaining a level of authority at United that saw him stamp his own personality on pretty much everything at the club. Sir Alex Ferguson *was* Manchester United, while the traditions and history of the club very quickly became a part of Sir Alex, something that stayed with him throughout his time at Old Trafford.

'Accepting change is really important,' he says. 'You should look at change. The way I addressed it was if someone gave me a paper that convinced me it was going to make us 1 per cent better, I'll do it, particularly the sports science. With video analysis I trusted my own eyes. I looked at it and used it for the players. We needed to in the sense that we'd break it down into what I said, and that's all you need to give them, because it was about us. When the video analysts showed me things, I knew all that because I'd seen all these players before. I'd been in management a long time, I trusted what I knew about my players and my opponents.

'My team talk when it came to opponents was, "Who's their best player, who wanted the ball all the time? Pay attention to that one," in terms of reducing the space or time he had on the ball. I never bothered about any of the rest of it. I talked about certain weaknesses. But it was all about our own team. I know more about my own team than I know about any other team. I think a lot of people rely on video analysis too much. It's important, the details are important, and if it helps you 1 per cent, do it. But I never made it my bible.'

Many people wondered what life would be like for Alex after he decided to retire, but he's as busy as ever with various engagements that fill up his diary months in advance. It strikes me that the work ethic that has always been such a feature of his life will never leave him. No matter what he does, that drive and enthusiasm come shining through. But there are some things that he misses about not being a manager, including the family feel he loved at the club.

'The buzz of the big games,' he admits. 'And you miss people, like the staff you had there, and the players and training. You miss that part, and I had a great staff – not just my own playing staff, but the people, the groundsman, the girls in the laundry, the girls in the canteen. When I went to United the stewards were all in their sixties – they were all older guys. They were hand-me-downs, from grandfather to father to son, and they were never paid. The way they were repaid was that if we got to the final they were all invited to the game for the weekend. If we didn't get to the final they used to have a big dinner at Old Trafford. Me and the staff all went. There'd be maybe 1,000 people there, and in a way they *were* the institution. They had a bigger tie to Manchester United than anyone, because they went back to their fathers and grandfathers. But then the law changed in terms of security and insurance, and they had to stop it. Today the stewards are all paid.

'My best period at United was every time I won the league, the first one and the last one, the European cups – these are the moments we're in it for. That's what I miss today, the big finals. You can't beat that, or the game where you win the league and you're waiting to see the results of other teams. The tingle you get from that.'

FOR A LARGE part of Alex's time Arsène Wenger and the various teams he produced as Arsenal manager proved to be among United's main rivals. Arsène took over at Arsenal twenty years ago, and his management has not only seen the north London club win Premier League titles and FA Cups, as well as consistently playing in the Champions League year after year. He has also been a major factor in building the club both on and off the field.

During his time he has produced great sides, including the 'Invincibles' of 2003–04, who went the whole season unbeaten as they won the Premier League title. He also oversaw the construction of a new training ground at the end of the 1990s and the club's move from Highbury to the Emirates Stadium ten years ago. When Arsène arrived in England the Premier League landscape was very different. Apart from Ossie Ardiles and Ruud Gullit, we didn't really have foreign managers in charge of our top clubs, and when he showed up at Highbury not too many people had heard of him.

'There was a lot of scepticism about foreign managers when I arrived,' he admits, 'because you had no history of successful managers from abroad and there was a kind of belief that foreign managers couldn't adapt here. There was a double scepticism about me because nobody knew who I was, and it was, "Arsène who?" I could see as well from the way the players looked at me that they were thinking, "What does this guy want?" One of the problems is that you always have to convince the players, but to start well you also need luck. And my luck was that I inherited a good team, players who were all basically over thirty, very experienced and very intelligent.

'I had Seaman, Dixon, Adams and Winterburn – they were all over thirty and they were winners – and I had players like Platt, Merson, Ian Wright and Dennis Bergkamp. It was a team. They were all experienced. The other good thing was that they had not made money. When I arrived it coincided with the TV money that was coming into the league. Ian Wright was a star and he was earning £250,000 a year, and from the time I arrived until a year or two later it went from £250,000 to £1 million. So when you are over thirty and suddenly you go from £250,000 to £1 million or £1.2 million a year, if you can gain one more year you're hungry. In fact, in British football we've gone from people who made their money after thirty to today, where they make their money before twenty! And that's a massive problem.

'So when I arrived I was able to convince the players that if they were serious, if they were dedicated, if they did my stretching and my preparation they would have a longer spell as a player. And I always gave them one more year, so the carrot was always there. They knew they had to fight for one more year. They were ready to die on the football pitch and that was my luck. They had the quality and they were hungry, and of course that helped. I believe when you come here from a foreign country you have to adapt to the local culture. You bring your own ideas, but you must not forget that you have to adapt to the culture.'

Part of the culture that confronted Arsène was something very different to what he had been used to. Back then it was still quite normal for players to enjoy themselves and go out for a drink after matches. They played hard and put the work in on the pitch, but then enjoyed themselves off it. It was still often a case of a team eating fish and chips on the coach when they were travelling back from an away game.

'I changed that, but the fact that we were winning and the players were getting bigger contracts helped,' he says. 'When you multiply your wages by four as a football player, that's not common, but they were intelligent and they were men. I did feel sometimes, "Are they going to be able to play on a Saturday?" I came from France where in training you worked hard, but on Saturday sometimes the players disappointed me. But I discovered here a generation that when the game started on a Saturday, they were competitors. I think you can play to play, you can play to compete – and you can play to win. These guys played to win. On Saturday they were ready absolutely 100 per cent to play to win.

'I slowly changed the diet, the training, and put across my ideas. I adapted a little bit as well, I changed things slowly and I encouraged my players at the back to play more. I came here with the idea that they could not play football, and that's when I discovered they were much better technically. It was a pleasant surprise because I encouraged them to play – and they liked it, they were capable of doing it. Bould, Adams, Winterburn – they were players, and I think we all met at the right time.

'I came here because of David Dein – he believed in me. I was lucky enough to meet somebody who gave me the chance to come to England and I will be grateful forever for that. He came a few times to Monaco when I was manager and we had a good relationship. Before I went from Monaco to manage in Japan I met with him and Peter Hill-Wood, but in the end they decided to go for Bruce Rioch as Arsenal manager. I went to Japan for a year and in the second year they came to see me and said, "We want you to take Arsenal." The most important thing in this job is to have good players. That's the only thing that matters, basically. No one can make miracles. I was lucky that when I came here I had a top team.

'What I like in England is the respect for tradition, but they are also crazy enough to innovate. It was surprising, but that's what I think I admire about this club – they have respect for the traditional values of the game and they keep them alive. But they took a French guy, who at that moment nobody knew, and there was no history of successful foreign managers in England. When I arrived it was nearly impossible to get a chance if you were foreign. I would say that today it's the reverse. It's much more difficult for an English manager to get a job in the Premier League than for a foreign manager. It was down to David Dein believing in me and giving me that chance.'

I can remember reading that Arsène had signed Patrick Vieira and then Emmanuel Petit on five-year contracts, and at the time it was quite unusual for a British club to be signing players from France or any other country, really, because we were pretty insular when it came to our football. With a few exceptions managers tended only to sign British players, so it all seemed very different, and not a lot of people knew that much about either of them.

'At that time, on the French market, I was alone,' he says. 'I could go and pick a good player and they were ready to come over to England with me. I knew Vieira from the French league and I had Petit as a player when he was at

Monaco. I thought at the time that they both had the physical stature – as well as the ability – to play in the Premier League. I remember when we went out in the tunnel before matches you had Bould, Adams, Petit, Vieira, Bergkamp, Ian Wright. They were massive, the guys were absolutely massive, and you won half the game before you went out. So at that time I could take from the French market what I wanted, and there were good players in France. Today, if you go to the French league there are forty-three scouts and twenty-five are English – so it's much different now.'

I was at Charlton as a manager for fifteen years, Alex and Arsène have even more years at one club, and I honestly can't see that happening again. Managing at any level, particularly in the Premier League and the Championship, is much more short-term now for a manager. If Arsène was walking into Arsenal today he probably couldn't afford to think beyond three or four years. That's the reality for a manager these days, and it's one of the big changes to have taken place during his time in England.

'Firstly, what has changed is ownership,' he says. 'When I arrived it was all local. The owners had bought "their" football club. They were fans as kids, were successful in life and then bought the club they loved. It's different today, it's an investment – and people are scared to lose their investment. We as managers are under pressure to be successful. It's a billionaires' club today.

'What you did at Charlton, and what I have done, is carry the values of the club through the generations, and you have that as a reference when a player comes in. I can say to the player, "This is the way we do things. We do this, we don't do that, you have to behave like this and not like that," because I've been here for a long time. If the manager changes every two years he's in a weak position to say things like that. The manager is not the carrier of the values of the club any more. I think it's very important that the values of the club are pushed through by the manager.

'I believe a manager has an influence on three levels. The first is on the results and the style of play. The second is the individual influence you can have on a player's career. Players can have a good career because the manager has put them in the right place, given them the right support, the right training. So you can influence people's life or career in a positive way, and the third is the influence you have on the structure of the club. I was lucky because when I arrived we had no training ground; we had Highbury, which is the love of my life, but it only had a 38,000 capacity. We got the training ground and the new stadium, and I was part of that, so that gives you a kind of strength as well. We had to pay back the debt. We knew we had limited money and we had to at least be in the Champions League to have a chance to pay off the debt.

'That was the most difficult period for me. For a while it was very bad, but today the club are financially safe. I personally believe the only way to be a manager is to spend the club's money as if it were your own, because if you don't do that you're susceptible to too many mistakes. You make big decisions and I believe you have to act like it's your own money. Like you're the owner of the club and you can identify completely with the club, because if you don't do that I think you cannot go far.'

To be at a club for as long as Arsène you of course have to cope with changes in the game and with things like the age difference that inevitably opens up when you're a sixty-six-year-old manager dealing with young players, some of whom are teenagers. He has needed to keep himself fresh, enthusiastic and motivated, as well as retaining the authority that any manager needs. So how has he gone about it?

'It's linked to the fact that you want to win the next game and you want to do well,' he insists. 'I believe you cannot stand still, you have to move forward. Look at Alex Ferguson – he was not scared to innovate, he did not stand still. I believe that if you want to stay a long time in this job you have to adapt to evolution. Today I'm more a head of a team of assistants. I manage the players, but I manage my own team as well. You have a big medical team, you have a big video team, you have a big scouting team, you have inside fitness coaches, outside fitness coaches. You know, when I first started and coached I was alone with the team and I was thirty-three years old. I was alone with them – and that's what I liked, that's what I've always liked. I like to go out every day. I don't like the office. I don't like paperwork too much. I like football to be more outside than inside.

'When it comes to the age gap with players, I try to speak about what matters to them. I cannot give them the last song of the latest rapper in the country, but what I can tell them is how they can be successful. That matters to them. With the difference in age I cannot act like I'm twenty, but what hasn't changed is that the boys try to find a way to be successful, and if I can connect with them in that way I have a chance. I have people who are more in touch with them, who give me the problems they have and then I can intervene at the right moment. But also if you are a young boy sometimes an older guy can give you reassurance on what matters to you. I try to do that – I say I can help them because I've done it before, and so they trust me. I believe what is for sure is that if you stay for a long time at a club, people have to believe that you're honest. That gets you through the generation gap, that's what I think is most important, because players don't expect you to be young when you're sixty-six. But they expect that when you say something, it's true. If they believe you are honest you have a chance.

'With authority, I think that some people have that naturally, and secondly as managers, we have the ultimate power – to play them or not to play them! On top of that, the player knows that if he wants to extend his contract he has to go through me. He cannot go to the chairman. That is massive. The player knows there's one boss and as long as you have that in a club, you have the strength.

'The more people you have inside the football club the more opinions you have. You have to have a good team spirit in the club, but everyone should just do their job. Do your job, and no more. Do not do the job of your manager. And sometimes when people stay a long time at the club, they have that tendency to have an opinion on everything. Do your job, don't intervene in what is not your responsibility and respect everybody else in his job. So we have to find a compromise between a family feeling and a respect that you don't do what is not your responsibility.'

So in those twenty years at Arsenal what have been the biggest changes for him?

'When I started the eye of the manager was the only data that was important, but today the manager is inundated with different types of information,' he says. 'He has to choose the four or five bits of information that are valid, that can help him to be successful. I believe the trend will be that the technical quality of the manager will go down and down, because he will be surrounded by so many analysts who tell him basically, "That's the conclusion the computer came to, that's the team you should play next Saturday." So we might go from a real football person to more a kind of head of a technical team.

'The power of the agent is another thing that has changed in the last twenty years. I've fought all my life for footballers to make money, but when you pay them before they produce it can kill the hunger. I'm scared that we now have players under seventeen, under eighteen, who make £1 million a year. When Ian Wright was earning that he'd scored goals, he'd put his body on the line. Now before they start they are millionaires – a young player who has not even played!

'What I do think will happen is that you will have more and more players coming out of the lower leagues who have had to fight their way through. Compare that with a player who has been educated here, who has had Champions League for seventeen years, who has not known anything else. So it's not a dream, it's normal for him, but if you play for a team in the lower leagues and watch Real Madrid or Barcelona on Wednesday nights you think, "I'd love to play in games like that." I've said to our scouts to do the lower leagues because the good players are there now. Don't forget we have many foreign players in the Premier League, but good English players have to go down to develop.'

Arsène's own hunger for the game and for management is very obvious when he talks about football. Like any manager he loves winning and absolutely hates to lose. The thought of retirement seemed a long way off when we talked, even though he knows it's inevitable one day.

'It's been my life, and honestly, I'm quite scared of the day,' he admits. 'Because the longer I wait, the more difficult it will be and the more difficult it will be to lose the addiction. After Alex retired and we played them over there he sent a message to me to come up and have a drink with him. I asked, "Do you miss it?" He said, "Not at all." I didn't understand that. It's an emptiness in your life, especially when you've lived your whole life waiting for the next game and trying to win it. Our pleasure comes from that – and our suicidal attitude as well!

'As people, part of us loves to win and part of us hates to lose. The percentage to hate to lose in me is bigger. Managers hate to lose, and if you don't hate to lose you don't stay for long in this job. If a match goes really well I might go out with friends or family for dinner or a drink. If it doesn't I'll go straight home to watch another football game and see another manager suffer. If we lose it ruins my weekend, but

I've learned over the years to deal with my disappointments and come back. What helps is when you come in, speak to your assistants, and then sometimes do a training session and start afresh. You could stay at home for three days without going out if you wanted to, but at some stage life must go on.

'The next game gives you hope again.'

All managers will be able to empathise with Arsène when he talks about losing. The despair of defeat for a manager is far greater than the joy of winning a match. When you win it's a relief and a time to briefly enjoy the victory that night, but even by the time you get in your car for the drive home your thoughts start to stray to the next match and what you have to try to do in order to win it. When you lose, that horrible feeling stays with you for a long time and it's hard to shake off. You'll replay the game over and over in your mind, thinking about what went wrong and what could have gone right. It doesn't matter how long you've been in the game, what you've won and achieved or how much experience you have. All managers experience very similar emotions.

THE MOST EXPERIENCED English manager in terms of the Premier League is Harry Redknapp, with more than 630 matches under his belt. Harry first became a manager in 1983 at Bournemouth, and in more than thirty years in the job has been in charge at West Ham, Portsmouth, Southampton, Tottenham and Queens Park Rangers. He's one of the best-known managers in the country, with bags of experience. He's always had an eye for a player and has always tried to fill his sides with footballers who have flair and are not afraid to express themselves on the pitch. He also rightly earned a reputation as one of the game's best man-managers and during his career was ready to take a gamble on some players who other clubs had given up on as they'd proved to be too much of a handful.

'The first thing I always look for in a player is that ability,' he insists. 'And then you think, "Yeah, I can get the best out of him." Those mavericks, if you can get them playing then you know you've got a fantastic player on your hands, and I enjoyed doing that. Di Canio at West Ham, Paul Merson at Portsmouth, Adebayor at Tottenham, young Ravel Morrison at Queens Park Rangers. You think if you can get them on side they can play, because they're fantastic foot-ballers. I always look for talent first and foremost, because I love people who can play. I would still take Adebayor again, I would still take Ravel Morrison because there's something about him. I loved his ability, and if I took a club now and could get him in I'd take him tomorrow. Talk about ability – I didn't know how good he was until I got him at QPR.

'I always think there's good in people, and I get on well with people. I look at them and think, "Come on, you're wasting your talent." I think that challenge of trying to get the best out of them is something I enjoy doing. I've always done it. Even at Bournemouth I had lads who could be a bit of a handful and at times it was hard work, but they did great for me when it came to playing and I loved that. You certainly have to handle players differently these days; managers can't shout and scream at players like some did years ago. Players don't respond to it and they can't accept it.'

Harry's ability to coax the best out of players and to put together entertaining teams has always been a trademark of his. His early days in management at Bournemouth in 1983 may have been very different to his time at QPR in more recent years, but he always applied certain principles to the way his teams played.

'When I started you went out and signed the lads on, there was no money and it was a struggle. Even something as basic as pre-season training was difficult. When I was at Bournemouth we never had a training ground. You'd go in the park and train. For one pre-season we found a field in the middle of nowhere that belonged to a little cricket club and they let us use it to train on. But we didn't have any facilities for food, so I used to go to a local supermarket in the morning to get some French sticks and my missus would make ham and cheese rolls for the players. When I was there it was you, maybe a coach, the physio and the kit man when you played away games, four of you, and everything was put into two baskets – shirts, shorts, the lot. Now when a team in the Premier League play an away game it's like you're going away for a year, with trucks full up with gear. I didn't know who all the people were when I was at Tottenham. There were people there on a Saturday and I didn't even know what they were doing there! We had so many masseurs, physios, analysts – so many people.

'I think it's completely changed for managers now. In the old days you'd do everything. You'd go and watch players, sign them, train them. You ran everything. That doesn't happen now. Agents don't deal with managers, they deal with chairmen and chief executives. They know managers are only passing through. I found at Tottenham that a player would very rarely come and see me about football. When a player had a problem they would talk to their agent, who would ring up the chairman and complain about me not picking them or something. The agent would be straight on the blower to Daniel Levy.

'I think the way managers have to operate now is very different. Like most managers, I used to go out and watch a lot of games looking at players. You'd go to a game and there'd be five or six other managers sitting in the directors' box as well, because we were getting all of our players from this country. Now they don't go to watch players. How can you when clubs are signing them from places like Argentina or Uruguay? Scouting systems are different now. You used to have a chief scout – he was the one who would bring players to you. Now so much of it is done by videos or whatever, because that is the way you get to look at players. If you get to go and see a player now it's a miracle.

'I think there was also a lot more contact between managers in the past than there is today. You would phone them and speak to each other more, and there was a camaraderie. When I was at West Ham we needed a striker. I remember going to watch a game in Scotland because I wanted to have a look at a particular player. When I got there the manager of this player saw me and actually warned me. He told me not to touch the player with a bargepole because he was a nightmare! There aren't many people who would do that nowadays, and it's very different for young managers.

'When I started I had some sort of grounding. It was a great experience, because you basically learned the ropes. Now, if you've played in the Premier League, to go and take a job in the lower leagues is very difficult, because you don't know the league and you don't know the players. I went to Oxford City with Bobby Moore years ago before I became a manager, and we never had a clue about any of the players at that level. It was different at Bournemouth for me. I'd played for them, I knew the level and when I got the job as manager I knew that division.'

So will players from the Premier League who want to go into management be prepared to learn their trade and cut their teeth at a lower level as Harry did before getting a crack at the top division, rather than expecting to get a job with a big club straight away?

'The problem is if a player has been earning £150,000 a week in the Premier League, is he going to take a job in one of the lower leagues for a grand a week?' asks Harry. 'He's earned more money in a week than he will in a year as a manager down there, and he's going to be thinking, "Now I've got to work all year for what I was earning in a week. And instead of getting home at two in the afternoon and having the day to myself, I've got to be out grafting!" It's difficult.'

Like all managers, Harry's had his ups and downs in the game. He did brilliantly at Portsmouth, getting the club promoted to the Premier League and then keeping them up against the odds, as well as leading them to victory in the FA Cup Final in 2008 against Cardiff. Another major highlight for Harry was leading Tottenham to a Champions League place in 2010 and taking them to the quarter-finals of the competition. The team he had then at Spurs, with the likes of Bale, Modric and Van der Vaart, was a really exciting one, and perhaps with another player or two they could have gone close to actually winning the title during the time Harry was manager at White Hart Lane.

'It was a great time for me and going into training was a pleasure,' he recalls. 'They'd be zipping the ball about, Bale, Modric, Van der Vaart, world-class players. It was a team. They'd have been up in the top four every year that group, but then they sold Modric and then after I left they sold Bale, but that was a good team. When I went in there in 2008 we changed some things around, pushed Bale forward and shoved Modric from wide left and put him in the middle of the park and his career took off then. Bale hadn't played on a winning Tottenham team for ages, but you always knew he was a fantastic talent.'

Harry lost his job at Spurs in 2012 but then went on to manage QPR, guiding them back to the Premier League after relegation, before deciding to resign in 2015. He's very much a football man who still loves the game, despite all the changes there have been, and through it all Harry's eye for a player and his natural ability to get them on side have never changed.

'I think players respond more to a pat on the back than someone shouting and screaming at them,' he adds. 'Bobby Moore once said to me that our manager at West Ham when we were players, Ron Greenwood, had never once said "Well done" to him. Bobby said we all need that in life, someone coming up to you and saying, "You were great today." People respond to things like that. Players do as well, and I think that's important.'

WHILE HARRY IS a vastly experienced manager, Chris Powell is at the other end of the scale. Chris played for me at Charlton and did a fantastic job. It didn't surprise me when he eventually went on to coach and then turned his hand to management. Ironically, his first full-time managerial appointment was at Charlton, where within the space of little more than three years he experienced both the success of getting the club promoted and the disappointment of losing his job when a new owner took over. Six months later he was back as a manager with Huddersfield, but his time there lasted just fourteen months before he lost his job. It's been a pretty steep learning curve for Chris, but despite the disappointment of losing his job twice, and knowing the pressures and stresses that go with the career, at the age of forty-six managing is still something he's determined to carry on doing.

'I think managers do the job because they love the game,' he insists. 'We all love the game. That's why I do it and it's why I want to continue doing it. When you go into it you have to be prepared for all the positives and all the negatives that the job will bring. We all have an expectation of how things will go when we take over a club, and you hope that things will go well. But you have to be prepared for the setbacks, and at the same time you have to have a go and put yourself out there. As a manager you're ultimately on your own – you make the calls and decisions, that's the manager's lot. Not everyone is going to be happy with the decisions you make, whether it's the players, supporters, the media, but you still have to have that inner belief that what you're doing is right.

'I think I always had it in my mind that I wanted to be a manager. I got the opportunity to coach when I was at Leicester, and that was invaluable because it was a great education to be involved every day and to see how the manager and coaches prepared, but there's not a thing in the world that can prepare you for being the number one. When you're a coach you think, "I can do that, I can be a manager." But it's when you actually become a manager and walk into the office on your first day with everyone there and looking at you, that's when you realise they're all thinking, "Right, what are you going to do?"

'When I was at Leicester I got a call to go for an interview at Charlton for the manager's job. Within twenty-four hours I was their manager, which felt great, but that's when everything else starts to kick in and you begin to appreciate how much the job involves. There's so much that you have to organise, and you soon realise that no matter what department in the club, it all comes to you. I think that was the biggest change for me. When I went to Charlton as manager they were in League One. As a coach you organise and do everything you need to for the day, and then you go home. As the manager that doesn't happen. You speak to the owner, you speak to the chief executive, you speak to the head of recruitment, you speak to agents – it never seems to stop. What you do have to do is try to organise some sort of time for yourself, but that in itself is hard to do because you want to do the job right, you want to do it well and you have to get involved in everything.

'One of the big things that hit me when I first got the job was when I walked out at the Valley for my first game there. I walked to the technical area, the whistle blew and I thought, "I'm leading this team now!" I'll never forget it. I turned round and looked at the dugout and the main stand during the game and thought, "This is it. You always said you wanted to manage. Now this is it." You stand there and you're really on your own.

'Winning as a manager surpasses winning as a player because it's the culmination of your work through the week, and to see it come together on a Saturday with a win, especially if the performance is to the levels you expect, it just surpasses everything. But if you lose it's terrible. There's no middle ground. It's so up and down, but as a manager you know that's in front of you when you take the job. You don't switch off, you're forever thinking about it. Managers are quite good actors – they'll say they're going out for a meal with their family to relax and enjoy themselves after a match, but all through that meal they're just thinking about the game they've just played and the next one that's coming up.

'I think the first six months I had at Charlton were invaluable. I had time to think about the next season and the restructuring I wanted to do with the team to try to get us promotion. We had a great start to that second season and didn't lose for twelve games. We got promotion and that was my first full season as a manager, so it was a big moment for me. The next season we were in the Championship, and you have to reassess and be realistic about what you can achieve as a newly promoted team – but we managed to finish ninth and were only three points off the play-offs. The season after I knew there were rumblings in the background about the club getting a new owner, and whenever there's a change of ownership it's very rare that you keep your job. It has happened, but it didn't happen with me.'

I suppose I was fortunate, because although I managed for seventeen years I was never actually sacked. But for most managers the reality is that the sack is really just around the corner, and for managers in the Championship their average tenure is about eight months, which is staggering. Managing in the Premier League is one thing and it brings its own set of problems, but managing outside of it can be very different. There isn't the money for clubs in the Championship or lower that there is in the Premier League, but everyone in the Championship would love to make that leap up to play with the elite and enjoy all the riches that come with it. As a consequence there's enormous pressure on a lot of Championship managers to achieve that goal and win promotion.

'The reality is that twenty-one teams in the Championship are going to fail every season,' Chris points out. 'Only three teams go up, and I think with lots of clubs short-termism comes into play. They want to get that success quickly, and maybe are not prepared to plan longer-term and build. I think as a manager you have a responsibility to try to bring young players through, to try to make that happen, but you also know that you're not always going to get time. That's the reality, and losing your job is something that every manager has to come to terms with. As a manager I think you should have a period of two or three months out of it when you lose your job. It gives you time to live your life a little bit, and mentally and physically get yourself back to where you should be because it's a stressful job. The stresses of running a club and dealing with different personalities is very tough on an individual. I think you need that break before you go back in. You always want to do things better next time and hope the people you work for are in line with you.'

Being a manager is tough for anyone, and what you do in your job is always under the microscope. You operate in an extremely public arena and your work is judged on a very regular basis. Chris is one of the few black managers we have in this country and as such I wondered if that brought any added pressures to what is already a very difficult job.

'To be honest I think the added pressure will always be there because it's such a big topic,' he says. 'It's an area where people have always wondered, "Why hasn't it happened more?" So I understand the position I'm in, and a few people who have been before me and who are in positions now. I understand how it is with regard to how I carry myself. I understand that people are looking up to me to see how I handle it, and that it may encourage others to become managers. Being a manager is a huge job regardless, but I've got a second job. I understand that to make a difference I have to do my job well. It may not always end up the way you want it to at a club, but as long as you've made a difference when you've been a manager at your particular club then that's good. I know people talk about the "Rooney Rule". That works – or has been working – in America. Maybe they've just got a bit more history in other sports like basketball; it's kind of been ingrained in the mindset of people for a long time there. We have to start somewhere and that somewhere is now. I think there are more black players thinking about coaching and managing, but I think maybe in the past there weren't too many people to look up to.'

Whenever I get asked about the job by a young manager and about how they should approach it, I always say that the first thing to do is get the expectation level right, from the chairman and from the board. What do they think would be a successful year on the budget they are going to give the manager? I think managing in the Premier League is totally different to managing in the Championship. The chances that come along for a young manager are few and far between. If you don't give it everything you'll regret it forever. You have to be totally consumed by it. As a footballer Chris played in all the divisions as well as for England.

He had the drive, ability and dedication he needed when he was playing, and hopefully those same qualities will see him have a long and successful career as a manager.

CHAPTER 2

PLAYER

Harry Kane, Mark Noble

WHEN FANS GO to watch their favourite teams and see the players walk out onto the pitch before the start of a game they are probably unaware of the different paths those footballers may have taken to get to that point in their lives. Being a first-team player doesn't just happen, and it certainly doesn't happen overnight. It has usually involved years of dedication, years of having to prove themselves and years of having to cope with the ups and downs the game will inevitably throw at anyone who wants to earn their living as a professional footballer.

Becoming a regular Premier League player can now offer financial rewards beyond most fans' dreams. Players are lucky to be playing in an era that offers these rewards, but they don't just walk into a top club's first team. There's a very long road that they have to travel that will test them mentally and physically, and even when they are part of a first team, it's up to them to keep proving themselves week in, week out. Very few players can afford to feel totally secure about their place in a team. Of course, you'd expect Messi or Cristiano Ronaldo to be the first name on the team sheet each week, but even they are not immune to injuries, and an injury can not only mean time out of a side – it can, in some sad cases, mean the end of a career.

Top players these days are the new rock or movie stars. They become household names, and are on the backs – and fronts – of newspapers. A lot of players get stick for the amount of money they earn and for not having the connection with the fans that players in earlier eras perhaps had. It's true that some of them don't do themselves any favours with the way they behave on occasion, but they are by no means the majority; a lot of players are hard-working, decent individuals who recognise how fortunate they are to be playing at a time when the game is awash with money for those who reach the top.

Our top division, the Premier League, has benefitted from all the big money, and there have been some big-name foreign stars who have graced the league and continue to do so. The temptation for clubs to widen their net when looking for talent has never been greater. The attraction of the Premier League means there are more than enough foreign players who are willing to play here, but that fact has also had a knock-on effect for young English talent, making it harder for our own youngsters to break through and reach the top. Later on in this book you will read about the dwindling number of English footballers playing in the Premier League, and one of the consequences of this trend is that there are fewer and fewer local kids who make it through to the first team with their local clubs and, more importantly, manage to stay there. In the past it was often the case that your club would have a few players in the side who had come through the ranks. They might even have been players who came from the same area you're from. That sort of thing seems to be happening much less now, and it's inevitable when you think of the footballing environment top clubs have to operate in. It's sad in many ways, but it's a fact of life.

So when you get players like Harry Kane and Mark Noble rising to the top, playing for the clubs they supported as kids and becoming local heroes, I think it's worth hearing about just how they managed to do so, and the trials and tribulations they had to overcome in order to get there. They strike me as being similar in many ways. They are honest boys from ordinary backgrounds who had the drive, determination and inner-belief to make it into their respective first teams and stay there. It goes without saying that they also had to have talent in the first place, but talent will only get you so far – there are plenty of stories to illustrate how some very good young footballers don't make it to the top.

I KNOW MARK quite well because I was his manager for almost two years at West Ham, but until recently I had never met Harry Kane. Like lots of other people I'd watched his rise to the top with Tottenham and England during the past couple of years, and was delighted to see it happen. He seemed to be a class act both on and off the pitch, with the talent and character that would take him a long way in today's game, and with that inner belief that helped him come through some trying times before he became the star name he is today.

'It was tough at times,' Harry admits. 'I first started training with the first team when Harry Redknapp was manager, and you think you're doing well and trying to get into the team, but in their eyes they're probably not even thinking about playing you any time soon. Football these days, with more foreign players that are being brought in, as a youngster you can feel you're on the cusp and then they might go and buy someone and you're back training with the reserves. For me it was just a case of being patient. I went out on loan. The first couple of loans – at Leyton Orient and Millwall – were good, and when I came back from them I thought I might have a chance of getting a run in the team, but it didn't really work out.'

Harry made his debut for the Tottenham first team in a Europa League match at White Hart Lane against Hearts five years ago and played a few more games in the competition for them. By that time he'd already had his loan spell with Orient and at the end of 2011 went on loan to Millwall. In the summer of 2012 Harry Redknapp left Tottenham and the club appointed André Villas-Boas in his place. A new manager presents a new challenge for any player because they naturally want to impress, especially if you're a young, nineteen-year-old striker, as Kane was at the time.

'I came back from the Under-19 Euros,' he recalls. 'AVB kind of said he wanted three strikers – two main strikers and another one – and he wanted me to be that third striker. I thought that would be perfect. I thought if I had a good pre-season I'd hopefully be in the squad for the Premier League games, maybe get some games and work my way into the team. But after pre-season I didn't really get into the team. He said it was probably better if I went on loan, which was a kind of setback. They also bought Clint Dempsey on the final day of the transfer window, so that was his third striker, and from my point of view it was probably another year where I wasn't going to be playing. And that's when I went to Norwich on loan.'

It was supposed to be a season-long loan but it didn't work out that way. As so often happens, Harry, like other players before him, had to deal with a season that produced some difficult times for him. He went to Norwich and got injured, breaking a metatarsal bone, which meant he went back to Tottenham for treatment before returning to Norwich. Then Spurs decided to recall him early from the loan spell, but after less than a month back at the club he was on his way again, this time to Leicester in the Championship for another loan period until the end of that season.

'That loan started okay, but then I found myself on the bench and that was tough,' he admits. 'It was the first time I was living away from home and it was the first real time I hadn't been playing. I was on the bench. My aim was always to go back as a Tottenham player and the loan was experience for me. But there were times when I was at Leicester that I thought, "I'm not even playing at Leicester. What are the chances of me playing in the Premier League any time soon?" There were doubts then that crept in, but I'm quite strong-minded and I thought to myself, "Look, be patient. You're young and things can change in football so quick." Even at that age I'd seen some careers go right up and then down. Some others had started slow and then come up, so I just knew I had to ride the wave and be patient.

'The season after that, which was AVB's second, I went on a pre-season trip to Portugal with the reserves and the first team went to Hong Kong, so I knew he wasn't looking to put me in his plans that soon. The trip to Portugal was one of the best things that happened to me. I went with Tim Sherwood, Les Ferdinand and Chris Ramsey, got really fit and played a couple of games out there, then came back and had a really good pre-season. I surprised AVB and he said to me that he wanted to keep me there, but then they sold Gareth Bale and were buying player after player. From my point of view it was tough, because you're doing well and thinking, "This might be my chance," and then they get all that money and start spending it on new players. It's another time where it tests your patience and how strong you are, how strong-minded you are. You could see all the players coming in, but I said to myself, "This is the season for me, I want to stay here and I want to prove that I'm good enough to be here. I don't want to go on loan." I didn't want to just go, take the easy option and get a few games. I wanted to stay and battle it out – so I did, and it was the best I'd ever trained. I was on fire. I had other first-team players coming up to me saying, "You'll be playing," but I wasn't getting any time. I was in the squad, but I was always nineteenth man. It was tough. I'd come home, talk to my family, talk to my agent. I'd think, "What else can I do? I'm the best player in training every day."

'My biggest fear was going on loan, and then someone getting injured and I'm not there. At the start of that season Emmanuel Adebayor was there, Jermain Defoe was there, Roberto Soldado had been bought and Dempsey was still there. AVB played one striker – you had four top strikers and they were big names as well. So never mind me not being happy to sit on the bench. None of them were going to be happy sitting on the bench! There were four strikers in my way, but I was adamant that I could get in front of them from what I saw in training. I knew that if I kept doing what I was doing, the older I got and the more physical I got, I was going to catch them up quicker than people thought. And that's sort of what happened.

'Adebayor wasn't really getting in the squad, so it left Defoe, Soldado and Dempsey. Obviously, I'm not stupid. I know what it's like when you're at a big club. I know they have the choice of who they're going to play – a £26 million player like Soldado, or me. I spoke to AVB about it. He was a nice bloke and I got on well with him, but he kept saying, "You're doing well. Keep doing what you're doing, you're young, just keep working hard." I'd heard that sort of thing before, but then things turn around quick, and it did that season. AVB left the job in the December and Tim Sherwood came in, who I'd spent a lot of time with. Him, Les and Chris came in, and I'd been with Chris since I was in the Under-15s and had a really good relationship with him. I was just coming back from a stress fracture of my back when Tim got the job, but I was obviously quite excited because it was a fresh start and Tim knew me. Whenever I'd spoken to him, he'd said, "You're good enough to be in the team," so I was excited. I was on the bench for a game at Old Trafford against Manchester United and he brought me on for the last ten minutes. I thought, "Here we go!" but although I got a bit of game time, even with Tim I struggled to get in the squad.'

At the end of that season Tim Sherwood was replaced by Mauricio Pochettino, who joined Tottenham from Southampton. I'd seen his Southampton team play and saw how he liked his sides to press high up the field. Tottenham by this time had sold Dempsey and Defoe, so when he first took over at Spurs my first thought was that Adebayor and Soldado would not be able to play the way he liked his striker to play. It just wasn't their sort of game, and that fact eventually proved crucial for Harry.

'When he came in I thought it was my chance,' he admits. 'There were only two strikers in front of me. I'd seen the way Southampton played, and thought, "That's me." I knew I suited his philosophy. I had a good pre-season – everyone was playing half a game, and I scored goals – but once again I couldn't get in that Premier League team. I played in the Europa League and was scoring goals, but I couldn't get in that Premier League side. I was getting minutes here and there, but then I came on in the game at Aston Villa in November and that was kind of the start of it.

'I've spoken to the manager about what happened at the start of that season and he asked me, "Why do you think you weren't playing?" I said, "I don't know, but obviously Adebayor was a big-money player, and they'd spent a lot on Soldado." He said that wasn't the reason. He told me that he knew I was scoring goals and doing well, but he didn't want to just throw me in ahead of Adebayor and Soldado and have people asking why they weren't playing. So he gave them the chance to play. They weren't doing what he wanted, so he brought me in. He said that Soldado and Adebayor couldn't then knock on his door and say, "Why are you playing this young kid in front of me?" He gave everyone a chance to play, but he always knew that I was going to be the one that he wanted playing. Because for him there was no rush. It wasn't like he'd come in and got six months to change everything. He knew he was building a team over two, three, four years. He's a great manager, the best I've worked under. People will say I would say that because he gave me my chance, but it's not that. It's the kind of all-round person he is. He's very smart. He's brave. He's not afraid of big-money signings, and he gets in and plays who he thinks is best. We've got a young team and I can only see us getting better. We're moving to a new stadium in a couple of years, so the future's very bright.'

Having finally made that breakthrough into the Tottenham side, Harry seemed to get better by the week, scoring goals for fun in that first season, getting thirty-one in all and twenty-one of them in the league, and taking seventy-nine seconds to score for England in his full debut against Lithuania. Not surprisingly he very quickly became a firm favourite with the Tottenham fans, with them singing the now-famous song about him, 'Harry Kane, he's one of our own' – that seems to be exactly what he is and why the supporters can so readily identify with him. To go from the relative obscurity of being a squad player with Tottenham to being their main man within the space of a less than a season could easily have had an unsettling effect on a young player, but that's not the case with Harry. He is a very down-to-earth individual who is both happy and grateful to be in the position he finds himself in.

'I'm a normal person and a big football fan,' he insists. 'I have a good family, good friends and a good agent. I always wanted this dream and I'm quite level-headed. There were times when it was tough, but to be in the situation that I'm in now is what I wanted. What it's about now is maintaining it, not taking my foot off the gas because I've got a nice house and I'm playing every week. I want to go on and win trophies. For me it's always about getting better and better. But it's different for me now, even walking down the street and people stopping you. Your life changes so quickly – and when you hit the international stage and you play for England, it doubles. But for me it's always been about getting better. It's having that inner drive and it's never been about the money – it's about winning trophies and playing on the big stage.

'There are rich teams out there and they pay their young-sters a lot of money. You do see youngsters who get ahead of themselves and you think, "What have you achieved to be doing this or that, to be driving around in that car?" If you're good enough and you're playing and doing well, you'll get more money than you could ever imagine anyway. You can't, as a fifteen-, sixteen- or seventeen-year-old be thinking, "I'm going to get loads of money," because to get that you've got to be doing well on the pitch. It's common sense that if you perform on the pitch and get better and better, money's not going to be a problem.

'Things are different for me now to when I first made my debut. Back then you didn't really know what to expect, walking out at White Hart Lane for the first time playing for the first team, and you want to impress and maybe you overdo things or try too hard. Now I've played plenty of games, and when I walk out there now I'm at home. It's about getting experience as a young player, which is why I think the loans were important. I didn't just come from reserve football to playing under the lights in a big stadium in front of big crowds.'

Having had such a good first season for Tottenham and at international level obviously meant there was pressure on him to perform right from the start of the 2015–16 season. There were comments and whispers about him possibly suffering second-season syndrome and not being able to turn it on again in the way that he had when he burst on the scene. Harry had to put up with mutterings about him being a one-season wonder from some people, and when he began the new season and failed to score in the league for Tottenham until the end of September there were whispers from some, questioning whether he was the genuine article. I never had any doubt that he was, and what impressed me about his play during that barren spell for him was his over-all play for the team. He never hid or shirked his responsi-bilities, and because he has the ability to drop off and play as a number 10 he's able to allow his teammates to go past him and can set up other people in the team. So even when he wasn't scoring he was influencing the game.

'It was always in the back of my mind – even at the end of that first season – that if I didn't score for two or three games, at the start of the next one people would say, "Second season. He's not going to do it again." Sometimes it was difficult,' he admits, 'when you're reading things maybe online or on social media, with people saying, "He's not as good as he was last year. He's not the same player." But I knew I was still playing well; it was just the goals that were the difference. I was doing well for the team, I was working hard for the team, so for me not a lot had changed except for the goals. I stayed positive and it wasn't like I was under pressure from the manager to score. He was happy with the way I was playing. I've always scored goals at any level I've been at, so I knew the goals were eventually going to come.

'Then things clicked and I managed to score quite a few in a row. It was a good moment for me – to prove everyone wrong and show that it wasn't just a one-season thing. I knew that I wasn't going to let that happen, but I did have something to prove and I stayed positive. But it does hurt you when people say, "Oh, he's not good enough. He's rubbish. It was a one-off season." It does hurt you – it would hurt anyone – but it gets that fire in my belly going and it makes you want to prove them wrong. When it did happen I wasn't going to say, "I told you so." I just got on with my business. I'd come home sometimes when I wasn't scoring and I'd be angry. I'd talk to my girlfriend and she would say all the right things, and I'd talk to my family and they would tell me to keep going, but that's what you need. You need to be able to let it out, and when things are going well you're all there together enjoying it. It's something I want to keep, and it's important to me to keep it throughout my career. There are bumps along the way that you've got to overcome, and having people who are close to you is important.

'A lot of people also talked about tiredness and having a rest after that first season, but I'm a player and I'd play every day if I could. In the summer when I went to the Under-21 Euros it was something I wanted to do for experience. It was the chance to go away in that sort of environment – the hotel life, the training, playing a game every three or four days – so for me it was getting experience for what was hopefully going to follow with England in Euro 2016. Obviously the Under-21 tournament didn't go as well as we would have wanted, but it was good experience and I never felt tired. I think a lot's down to the manager and staff at Tottenham, because they're very good at knowing when the time's right to have a rest and when to train hard. We're probably one of the only clubs to do double sessions throughout the season, but the staff and management keep me fresh and healthy. It would take quite a lot to stop me going out and playing. I feel like if I didn't play because of a little injury I'd be letting people down and letting the team down.

'I want to play in every game, but obviously if the manager rests me and puts me on the bench he has his reasons. I would never say to him, "Look, I want to be playing." It's his decision and I go with it. When I'm on the bench I think about what it was like at Leicester – I'd be on the bench and used to think that if I got the chance to go on I'd have to change the game. You've got to have that mentality – to make an impact when you come on and make a difference.'

One of the things I've noticed with Harry's goals is the way a lot of them come because he gets his shots off so quickly. He doesn't take an extra touch that a lot of strikers do, and because of that defenders – and more particularly, goalkeepers – don't have a chance to get themselves set. I wondered where he'd got the technique from.

'That was Defoe,' he says. 'He was the best I've seen at that in training. He was unbelievable. We'd play little games or five against five, and he'd get the ball, touch and finish! He used to score so many goals by doing it. If defenders closed him down and got tight, he had the ability to skip past them. I think it's important for a striker, especially in the Premier League, to get shots off early, because defenders will get back in time and block the ball, and keepers these days are so good they'll see it coming and block it.'

Like all strikers, and despite his all-round team play, Harry lives for goals. His path to the top, and the way he had to persevere and believe in himself, should be an inspiration to youngsters out there who are trying to battle their way through and are suffering some inevitable knockbacks along the way.

'I hope what happened with me can give younger players that drive and that goal to go and get in the first team,' he says. 'Things can change so quickly for you in football, and for me patience is a big thing. There are probably times when you think you should be playing in the first team, but being patient and not letting it get to you is a big part of it. I do see myself as quite an older figure at the club even though I'm still young. But we have a young team and a lot of younger players coming through. You can see times when they get frustrated, when they get left out of squads and things like that. I've said to a couple of them, "Just be patient, your time will come, you'll get your chance. Just be ready."'

Harry's connection with the club and with the Tottenham fans is genuine and something that he is happy to have. There is nothing better for a fan than to see one of the club's youngsters make it all the way to the first team and be successful, because so often over the years that has not been the case and, as I have mentioned, the competition for young English players to make it all the way to the top has never been fiercer. So it's good to see a success story like Harry's and it's fantastic for the Spurs fans to know they are watching 'one of their own' who is delighted to be playing for the club.

'I've been at the club so long, since I was eleven years old,' he says. 'I've been to games – I was a fan watching games before I was a player – and I know what it's like to be a football fan. I'm a big football fan. I think the fans appreciate the way I work for the team and put in my all every game, and you get that connection with them. Obviously they sing the song about me, and I just try to give something back to them. Fans are a big part of football. If you don't have fans you don't have football. So I think it's important you take time out for them. It's got to work both ways – they come and support you, and you've got to support them as well. You have that connection and that feeling with the fans, where you probably wouldn't want to go anywhere else. You have that good feeling. Every game they're singing your name and cheering you on. Why would you want to go and start somewhere else? If you've got that connection, that's what you want in football.'

HAVING THAT SORT of connection with the fans was something I witnessed first-hand when I was Mark Noble's manager at West Ham, and it was no surprise that his was the biggest-selling shirt in the club shop. Like Harry Kane, he had to go out on loan and then had the belief and strength of character to say no to another loan in order to battle it out and earn himself a place in the first team. That was when I first came across him as a young player.

'I'd been out on loan at Hull and at Ipswich,' he recalls. 'The manager at the time was Alan Pardew and I was eighteen years old. I went up to Hull and didn't enjoy it. I did my back in the first training session I had with them. I carried on and played some games for them, but I didn't enjoy it. The next season I went out on loan to Ipswich and I loved that, and I remember coming in from a training session one day and seeing that West Ham had signed Carlos Tevez and Javier Mascherano and thinking, "Where has that come from?" I came back from that loan and went to see Pards in his office. He said, "I'm going to send you out on loan again," and I said I didn't want to go. If I'm honest, the team were in trouble and it looked like he was going to get the sack. So I thought, "I don't want to go on loan for three months, he gets the sack, and then when I come back nobody knows who I am." So I took a chance and stayed.'

Alan Pardew did get the sack, and I was the man who took over. Mark had played a handful of first-team games before I arrived but wasn't an established first-team player. He impressed me when I got to West Ham – he was in my face every day, desperate to be in the team, and he trained the way he played, giving everything. I began to play him in the team as we successfully battled against relegation, winning seven of our last nine league matches, and Mark then became an established member of the first team during my time at the club.

'I always believe the decision I made to say I didn't want to go out on loan again saved my career at West Ham, for sure,' he says. 'That decision was probably the best I've ever made and I've now played more than 330 games for the club and I hold the record for Premier League appearances for them, as well as having been through some amazing times with them. I think what happens with so many players now is that they haven't got the self-belief. They go out on loan, and the next minute they're forgotten about. They might play in the Championship and forget about what it means to be a Premier League player. I think you can go out and you're happy, but you sort of lose that will to say, "No, I'm going to play in this team."

'One of my proudest achievements as a player is that I've had five or six different managers during my time at West Ham, all with their different ideas and different ways of playing – and from different cultures – but I've started every season in their teams. I know I'm not the greatest player in the world, but I know I'm a good player. I know I've got ability, but I know my enthusiasm, hard work and commitment to playing probably outweigh my ability in some ways. I class myself as a good Premier League player who's played a lot of games and knows what the league is about. When a new manager comes in to the club you have to reinvent yourself in some ways and think about how he wants you to play, and then get on with it. That's where your mental strength and willingness to learn come in. That's when you have to impress the manager and say, "Right, I'm going to be in your team." I think that kind of thing is born in you, having that self-belief, and I've always wanted to play for the club.

'I think it has a lot to do with how you're brought up and where you're brought up. I was born in Newham General Hospital, a golf shot away from Upton Park. I went to school in east London and used to go and watch games at West Ham before I ever played for them. I've seen loads of players with the natural ability to get to this level and play in the Premier League but who mentally can't cope with what you have to do, especially once you get into the team. So to get there and stay there and to keep playing at that level, to overcome a bad game or a 3–0 loss, or getting abused by the fans, you have to be mentally able to cope with that – and not a lot of people can.

'You speak to players now and a lot of them say, "You've got to get a move to earn the money, to get appreciated." Obviously when I was young I wanted to earn money, like every young kid does when they're a player, but I've always really enjoyed that fight, that challenge of saying, "They've bought him or him, but there's no way he's playing me out of the team!" I use it as motivation. I always think, "Right, it's my spot and you're not taking it." You get some players out there and they don't play and they're fine with that, but I've never been able to enjoy not playing. To be honest, I've never really been able to enjoy life if I'm not enjoying football. It's probably wrong, because at the end of the day it's a job and I work for West Ham. It's a great job, but if we lose on a Saturday everything's affected for me. Everything. For a lot of players it doesn't affect them, but it affects me – you just ask my wife. It affects the way you live, especially me. If I don't play well or we get slaughtered, it's horrible.'

Mark has been playing in the West Ham first team for ten years now, and the fact that he has maintained his place in the side under so many managers is testimony to how much each of them have rated him. His consistent performances make him one of the first names on the team sheet each week, and he has proved himself to be a quality player operating in one of the best leagues in the world. He has seen quite a lot of change in the game during his time at the club and believes that players like him may soon become a dying breed in the Premier League.

'I talked to my teammate Aaron Cresswell last season and said that players like us – who are not really that fast, not really that strong, not really that tall and not really that athletic, but are good English footballers – we'll be gone soon! The reason is that clubs can go and buy a foreign player for £2 million. If you look at me now, I'm twenty-nine years old and I might be worth, say, £8 million in the transfer market. So if a club were looking, would they spend that money on me or someone like me, or would they go abroad and get four players for the same price? There's a much bigger pool for clubs to look at when they want a player now to the way things were even ten years ago. Probably ten or twenty years ago West Ham might have had a European scout. Now we've got scouts all around the world looking at players. No player who's doing well goes unnoticed.'

Mark's strong connection with the area the club are based in and with the fans has made him a firm favourite with them. But I know from personal experience that it isn't always easy for local lads. I regularly used to go out for a meal with a couple of friends, Glen and Lee, who I first met when we were all apprentices. I was at West Ham, Glen was with Ipswich and Lee was at Chelsea. We're still friends to this day, but when I was manager of West Ham and we were battling against relegation when I first took over, they told me they couldn't go for one of our regular get-togethers because the restaurant we went to was in the heart of West Ham territory – and they knew the evening could be spoiled by me getting stick from fans! Mark has had to deal with that sort of thing throughout his career, but knows it goes with the territory.

'I've got four or five close mates from school and they're still mates now,' he says. 'When you're brought up in the area then everyone you know is an East Ender and all their friends are from the East End as well. Sometimes someone will ask for twenty shirts to be signed and you can't really say no, because they're friends of friends – or you'll get asked for twenty tickets for a match. Sometimes when it's not gone right, and believe me there have been times at West Ham when it's not gone right, you'll see people in the street and they'll be wanting to know what's gone wrong and what's going on at the club. I've always answered questions straight and I've never thought about not going somewhere because I might get pestered. It's because people love their football so much that they want to know what's happening. The game is so big now and every match in the Premier League is televised. So if you misplace a pass or make a mistake, that's highlighted three or four times during the week.

'I love being a footballer, and for me it's a pride thing not a money thing. Some fans might see you lose 3–0 and think, "Look at the amount of money they're on. I'd lose 3–0 every week for that amount!" But it's not the money. If you care, like I do, it's pride. I want to be able to walk down the high street and have fans say to me, "Well done, Mark. Good game on Saturday." You want that instead of hearing them asking you what the hell is going on at the club and telling you to sort it out. It's a pride thing, and the money doesn't come into it for me. Of course, it's great that I've got nice things now – and I've worked hard for them – but when we lose on a Saturday I don't walk off thinking, "I get paid next month." That doesn't come into your mind. You think about the next game and you want to get a result from that game. You think about winning. You might lose four on the bounce, but then you get a win and you start thinking, "We're all right!"

'Once I've stopped playing and I look back at what I've achieved, I know I'll be pleased. I've gone from being a little kid growing up in east London to being the West Ham player with the most Premier League appearances for the club, being involved in some big games for them like the two play-off finals, having a testimonial last season and captaining them in probably the biggest year in the club's history as we move from Upton Park into the new stadium. I know I'll be proud of what I did as a player.'

CHAPTER 3

LEGEND

Rio Ferdinand, Steven Gerrard,
Frank Lampard

THE WORD 'LEGEND' can be a bit overused in football, but when it came to looking at players who I felt had truly earned that status, three immediately sprang to mind – Rio Ferdinand, Steven Gerrard and Frank Lampard.

I always think that there has to be a very important ingredient in the character of any player who makes it to the top in the world of professional football. Talent can only get you so far in the game if you're playing it at the very highest level. Of course it's important if you are going to have a long career, but there is something else all the top players have – and without it they wouldn't be half as successful as they are.

They have to have hunger.

I know a lot of people think players these days have it easy, that they get paid ridiculous amounts for kicking a ball around and for doing something fans can only dream of, but believe me, being a professional footballer in the Premier League is not easy. Yes, of course the rewards are vast, and they are fortunate to be playing in an era when the money in the game is so plentiful, but they can't be held responsible for that. I'm sure that when I played in the 1970s and 1980s there were people saying the same sort of thing, because although the rewards were nothing like they are now, they would still have been huge in comparison with the wages of players thirty years earlier.

The fact is you don't choose when you are born, and all you can do is get on and make the most of what's on offer during your time. Everything has got bigger and bigger in the Premier League. When it first started twenty-four years ago people thought the money the league was getting from TV was incredible. The sums were vast and like nothing else that had been seen before. They got £25 million over three years back then. It's now around £8 billion over three years for domestic and international TV. The figures are almost incomprehensible, and there is a worldwide hunger for the product that is the Premier League. Of course the players have benefitted, but you can't blame them for saying yes to big contracts if they are on offer.

* * *

AS A PROFESSIONAL you play football and get paid for it, and you only get to do that in the first place because you have the ability to perform at a high level. There are various degrees of ability in our game, and there are some very good players who will never make that breakthrough into the really big time and play Premier League football. All professionals have to be of a certain standard, but those who make it into the Premier League and then perform consistently at that level week in, week out are the elite. To do that for a season or two, or even three, four or five years on the bounce is tough, so to do it for eighteen years and for the most part with a team who were at the very top of the English game is pretty remarkable. But that is exactly what Rio Ferdinand did.

During the course of the Premier League history he has been one of its major players, consistently turning in performances of the highest quality, and apart from his undoubted ability it is Rio's hunger that has been a mainstay of his fantastic playing career.

He was a big part of the league for all but four years of its existence during his playing days, making his professional debut for West Ham in their last Premier League game of the season, against Sheffield Wednesday in May 1996. He was just seventeen at the time, and went on to become one of the best centre-backs this country has ever produced.

He was always a very good ball-playing defender, and during his early career was just as comfortable playing in midfield. As a kid growing up in south London Rio was football mad, and his talent shone through at a very early age. All of the clubs in the area – and many beyond it – were aware of him, but it was West Ham who eventually got lucky and signed him. He joined them when he was thirteen, progressing through the ranks before making that first-team debut four years later.

You always knew he was going to be a player because he was not only very talented, he was also a natural athlete, and that is something you have got to be in order to play and compete at the very top. I remember seeing him in a youth-team match when I was managing Charlton and he was playing in midfield for West Ham. He looked very comfortable on the ball, was able to see a pass and could tackle. Even at that early age there was also a calmness and assurance about his play, something that was to become a hallmark of his as the years went by. When he later dropped back to play in the centre-half role he was able to do so knowing he had tremendous pace, which not many centre-backs have, and his class was evident.

From as early as he can remember Rio always wanted to be a footballer. He had the skill, ability and dedication to make that happen, and his hunger to do well and achieve things as a player never left him. When he talks about growing up as a football-mad kid you really get a sense of just how happy and grateful he is that he was able to fulfil the dreams he had as a youngster.

'When I was growing up me and my mates all used to say that if we played one minute of professional football we'd all die happy,' he says. 'It didn't matter whether it was going to be in Division Three or Four, as they were in those days.

At least I then knew I would be able to go out and say, "I've played professional football." It meant that much to us then, and it still means so much to me today.

'I just used to love playing football, and I'd go out and try to play like Gazza, John Barnes, Paul Ince, Frank Rijkaard or Maradona, all the big names of that time – and they were the players I admired most. I wanted to play just like them, and I'd go out in the street, have a kickaround with my mates and try to do just what I'd seen them do. It wasn't like it is today, where every kid knows everything he wants to know about a player – because there is so much information out there. My little ten-year-old son knows all there is to know about the top players, from the way they look and play to what they have to eat for breakfast. Back then all I really knew about those players was the way they played, and that was good enough. It captured my imagination, and football meant everything to me.'

Having played at the top for such a long time and in an era when the Premier League has got bigger, better and stronger, Rio was at the centre of a globally popular competition that shows no signs of diminishing. During his time as one of its major players he saw the league and all those involved in it change and develop into what it is today. His footballing memories and background are, in many ways, from a very different time, but he played and grew with the league, seeing the changes it has brought to clubs, players and fans. He won pretty much all you could at club level, as well as captaining his country, and he knows just what it's like to be a top player in the modern game. Throughout his distinguished career his hunger seems to have been at the core of the success he enjoyed.

'I think I always had a work ethic when it came to my football,' he insists. 'That came from my parents. My mum worked with other people's kids and was always there to make sure we had the nice things every now and again. My dad used to travel from north London to south London to take me to west London for training, so I always knew that I had to be ready; I couldn't mess about, because I realised what a big effort he'd made to take me to training. I was lucky because I had a district manager called Dave Goodwin, who used to say, "Set targets for yourself." I always did that as a kid.

'When I was at West Ham he would ask me what I thought I could achieve at certain points. So I'd say things like, "Being a regular in the youth side and then maybe get six or seven appearances in the reserves during my early days at the club." When I'd reached those goals I set myself new ones. I was always trying to push myself to do better and achieve more from a very early stage, and that sort of approach to my career never really left me. I was never satisfied to just sit back and be content with what I'd done, because as far as I was concerned there was always more to do.

'I think kids now can get a bit wayward. They get to a certain stage and they down tools. I've known loads like that throughout my career. I'd have been embarrassed to go home to my mum and dad and my mates on the estate I grew up on, say I'd played two games for a top club and then never be seen again. It would have killed me. I'd have moped around, and you wouldn't have seen me. I was always serious about what I did when it came to football.

'Things are different now. I think with some young players, they get their first contract, they know it's been in the press and that people know who they are. They'll maybe get into nightclubs for free and they start to think about all sorts of things. For them it's more about what comes with being a footballer, rather than being a footballer.

'I always say to young kids, "You're going to get rich, you're going to get access to all sorts of things – if you work hard. All of that comes along naturally, but you have to work hard." They might crave the money and everything else, but at the same time forget the hard work that goes into making sure all of that happens.

'That's why I give so much credit to Ronaldo. He wasn't the finished article at all when I first knew him, even though he had great ability, but his drive and desire to be a top player were always there – and it's just the same now. I spoke to Gareth Bale about him a while ago and he said that Cristiano was relentless. That every day in training he always wanted to win, he always wanted to score. It's just the same as when he was at United. He hasn't changed – he's still really driven, still wants to keep working even though he's the best player in the world.

'It's about taking pride in what you do as far as I'm concerned, and that has always been part of me. I always wanted to earn respect from people, whether it was a football manager or someone you were playing against in the park. I wanted them to think, "That Rio's a good player." That's all I've ever cared about.'

After his start in professional football with West Ham, Rio went on to play 127 games for the club before being transferred to Leeds United as a twenty-year-old for a record £18 million fee. He then moved on to Manchester United in the summer of 2002 for another record fee, this time £30 million, making him the world's most expensive defender and the most expensive British footballer at the time. It was at Old Trafford that he enjoyed his greatest success, playing for fourteen seasons and winning the Champions League, six Premier League titles, three League Cups and one Club World Cup. He also played eighty-one times for England and captained his country in the process. His transfer to Queens Park Rangers in the summer of 2014 meant that Ferdinand played in twenty-one Premier League seasons, and he'd seen it change and evolve into what it is today. Rio had to change and adapt as well, and the dressing-room culture these days, particularly at the big clubs, is light years away from what used to go on.

'Everything about the league has changed during the time from when I started until I finished,' he says. 'The diet of players, the scientific methods used to track what players do and the way you perform. It's all monitored now, and there's no escape from it or getting away with things. The pace of the league is different now as well. The speed and quality are massively high. The fitness levels are obviously better, but it's the quickness of the game and the fact that any mistakes are usually punished with a goal, or at least a shot on goal, that are really the major features. Years ago as a player at West Ham if I'd wanted to coast through a training session I could probably have got away with it. That couldn't happen now. When I went to Leeds the challenges there were a bit harder and the targets different, and then when I moved to Manchester United they were even harder – and so were the demands.

'When I started at West Ham and got into the squad it was a case of "all-dayers" on a Tuesday, all out on a Saturday night and sometimes "all-dayers" on a Sunday as well. Because they're all at it you could get away with things if you wanted. You could think, "I feel tired today," but then there were ten others feeling the same!

'If you did that sort of thing at Manchester United you were one on your own and you stood out like a sore thumb. You wouldn't be playing for a month and pretty soon you'd be on the scrapheap, or off somewhere else to a lower-league team. So the change in dynamics was huge.

'Partying and socialising were a big part of my life at West Ham when I was a kid, even when I got into the first team, but when I was at Man United that all changed. If anyone had seen my day-to-day existence when I was at Old Trafford they would have thought it was really boring. I'd finish training in the mornings, go home, go to sleep for an hour or two, wake up, get the kids from school, then go back and sit in the house watching TV or whatever. People think you're always out – that you'd go to the opening of an envelope or you're at a party. They think you have an extravagant lifestyle, but believe me, if I had done those things I wouldn't have been at Man United for long.

'I know a player who was the first in my year group to break into the first team. He had terrific ability, but his life-style probably didn't change from when he was sixteen years old to the day he retired. He was always out drinking, and that never left him. He had the talent, but other players who weren't as good as him went on to have better careers.

'The environment you're in can play a part. At Leeds there was a drinking culture when I was there. We had lots of young lads in the team and the city was based around Leeds United Football Club. We were the form team and it was an exciting time to be there. I was in that drinking culture, but I was still being more professional than I'd been at West Ham. I was maybe only going out twice a week instead of four times. My performances were going well – and at that age you can get away with it – but when I went to Manchester United it was a much more mature squad. I remember look-ing at people there and thinking, "I'd better start doing what they're doing." The number of games we were involved in demanded that you had to do things right. We were playing top games three times a week sometimes, so you just had to knock all the socialising on the head or you weren't going to be able to perform and compete at that level.

'If you look at a typical week when you're involved in the Champions League, there's no way you could perform if you didn't do things right. You might be at Newcastle on the Saturday, so you'd have to travel up there on the Friday. After the game you'd travel home and then be in at the training ground on the Sunday for a warm-down. Monday would be a normal training session and then on the Tuesday, let's say, you'd fly off for a match in Turin. You'd play the game on the Wednesday, and if you were playing away again on the following Saturday you might stay an extra night in Turin and come back on the Thursday. Then on the Friday it would be travelling to wherever you were going to be playing on the Saturday, so there'd be another overnight stay in a hotel before the match the next day. When you play for a top club there's no time for messing around.

'Mentally and physically you have to get yourself in tune for a match. The great thing about it is that there's such a quick turnaround of games, so if you're down emotionally it doesn't last long. The thing at United was that you didn't lose two on the bounce. That was what we always said. So if you lost once you had to get back up and make sure you didn't lose another one. I always liked playing games and it makes the season go quicker.

'It took me years, probably until I was twenty-six or twenty-seven, for me to really understand what I was doing, how I needed to get myself up for games. I used to visualise things before matches, visualise what I wanted to do and then play the game. I also tried to make sure I didn't beat myself up if we were losing – and I never got too high when we were winning. I think that was the thing about Manchester United, that's why we were able to maintain that level of consistency for all those years.

'One of the other things we did was never celebrate too hard when we won. When we lost – things like European Cup Finals or FA Cup Finals – they were probably the best nights we had drink-wise. The attitude was, "Let's just forget that, the match is gone." When we won things it was all about saying, "Right, next year we'll be back again and we've got to win it again."

Although Rio is still only thirty-seven, a lot of his football background was formed in a very different time. Lots of what he did as an apprentice coming through the ranks at West Ham, I did when I was there as a young player in the 1970s. There were no academies when I was a youth player, and the menial jobs you had to do were just part of the whole process, something that I didn't particularly like but that I never had a problem with. One of the jobs I had to do was cleaning the brass handles on the doors at Upton Park, and when Rio went there he had to get used to doing similar things, as well as trying to make it as a professional.

'The kids don't do jobs these days, and if you ask for anything they look at you as if you're mad,' he says. 'I used to do all sorts of jobs when I was a kid at West Ham and I also had to clean the boots of striker Tony Cottee and the manager, Harry Redknapp. I didn't like doing the jobs, but you got on with them and you knew that the only way of getting out of them was to become a professional. The minute I signed pro forms I didn't have to clean the gym any more. The other players would be saying, "He's not doing his jobs." The coach would say, "He's training with the first team. You start training with the first team and you won't have to do jobs either!"

'It's changed a lot when it comes to the youngsters at clubs. If you go and watch a youth-team game now a lot of players are manufactured. A lot more young players are like robots. The street-footballer type of player is something I don't think you'll get any more. There'll be the odd one or two who are different, but I think it's the way the clubs go about things – they turn out these robot players. It's as if they're churning out digitally programmed footballers. They all do the same type of turn and they all try to do the same sort of pass. Some of the managers now don't really think about the player. They just want people who fit into the system and you think, "Surely there's got to be a bit of scope, a bit of individualism?"

So considering the way in which he feels kids are treated these days, would he want his son to follow in his footsteps and become a professional footballer?

'I'd love him to be a footballer. That would be my dream, him playing professionally at a decent level. But it's hard. I grew up in a society where your mum basically just threw you out the door, and you had to go off to find your mates to go and play football. Now, if my son wants to play football with a friend's kid there are phone calls involved and we have to organise things. It's not the kid's fault, it's just that it's not the same any more. So for my son to just go off and play football, it's not the same as it was for me. The environment he lives in is different to the one I had. The kids have a lot more ways of seeing football and learning about players and skills, with iPads, Xboxes, all sorts of things. It's a different world.

'But I still think that it's important to motivate them. My son has gone to games and I've asked him if he wanted to one day play on a pitch like Old Trafford. I've told him that if he does want to, then he has to work hard otherwise it won't happen. I've let him go on the pitch for two minutes and I could see what it meant for him. He told me how much he loved the smell of the grass, and I thought to myself, "He's actually starting to feel it," the excitement and buzz you get from the thought of playing football on a pitch like that. It's exactly the same thing I had. I'd smell the pitch and imagine myself cutting out a few little passes on the grass. It's all part of the excitement playing football can give you, and I'd love it if he became a player.'

It strikes me that Rio's motivation as a player was always to just play football. It may sound simple and uncomplicated, but that's just what it was. He didn't become a professional because he dreamed of making loads of money, having fame, nice cars and nice houses. He did it because he wanted to achieve things as a footballer, and all the other things have followed on. If his son does make it as a footballer and plays at the same level as his father, the professional game will be a very different place for him from the one his dad first entered.

Although I made the point earlier about a professional not being responsible for the fact that the money on offer these days is so huge, there is no doubt the sums involved have changed the modern game. I remember Alex Ferguson once telling me that one of the biggest problems he had at United was when all the young boys who had come through the system became first teamers, because it also meant they basically became millionaires. He was worried that because of the money they might lose that hunger and aggression, but of course he managed them really well and in the end it never had a bad effect. I think Rio and many of the players from his particular era would still play football if the money was the same as it was twenty-five years ago. A lot of players now get fantastic contracts when they are just nineteen or twenty years old. They think it's normal, whereas people like Rio, who have earned good money from the game, understand just how hard it was to get that money.

He also has an understanding of what the fans mean to the game. He grew up at a time when supporters could go in a pub and have a chat with the players they'd been watching on the Saturday afternoon. That has changed now, but he still understands the need to keep in touch with them and has used things like social media to do just that, with nearly six million people following him on Twitter.

'I think in many ways the connection between players and fans has gone, and I think a lot of that is down to the money, and the way the modern game is these days with the intensity and concentration on fitness levels,' he admits.

'Whenever there's some sort of argument or dispute concerning a player, the first thing that comes up is, "He's on X amount of money – why doesn't he just shut up and play?" To a certain extent I can understand that, but sometimes it's a bit more than just going out and playing because of the money you're earning.

'Let's say a fan hears that a player is feeling a bit tired because he's playing three games a week. They can't understand that. They think, "He's on £100,000 a week, how can he not want to play? I'd play with my leg hanging off for that!" I know it's hard for fans to understand that, but if you look at it another way, if a player feels he's not up to playing then he'd be doing a disservice to the team and the club by just turning out and not performing at his best. When Raheem Sterling said he was tired while he was on England duty and wasn't right to play he got a load of stick for it. I actually think if a few more of us had done the same thing over the years – people like Rooney, Gerrard, John Terry, Ashley Cole and myself for example – England might have had a better chance in some of the tournaments. But we were all too proud. It was the old English mentality that we had to be out there on the pitch, even if we weren't right.

'I do think it's important to stay in touch with the fans, to maintain a connection. It's not as easy as it was – the world is different now – but that's why things like social media are important. When I was a kid I wanted to know exactly what players were doing – where they were eating, sleeping, whatever. I wanted to know everything I could about them. That's why I go on social media now, so that people can see what I'm doing and there can be some connection.

'I realise that footballers are role models – they have to be, they've got no choice. I found it hard when I was younger, having that sort of responsibility, because all I wanted to be was a professional footballer. I didn't understand it. I didn't play football to have responsibilities to a lot of kids and the general public, and I made a lot of mistakes growing up. But then after a period of time you begin to understand a bit more.'

That level of responsibility and being in the public eye is something all modern Premier League players have to accept, and the celebrity that goes with being a player these days has never been greater. Whether they like it or not, the modern-day player is like a pop star, and they have to learn to deal with that and adapt their lives accordingly. Rio has been around long enough to know how to cope with that side of things, and at the same time try to keep his private life private.

'As a footballer you learn to get used to things like not having proper Christmas Days with the family or missing out on family holidays and birthdays. It's just the way it is,' he says. 'I never went around looking for things that put me in the spotlight. That's why I don't do *OK!* or *Hello!* magazines. I played football, had a great time, and it's given me a great lifestyle, but my family don't have to be a part of that. I recognise the fact that people might want autographs and things when I'm out with my family, and you just have to manage it.'

Rio was always a 'proper' player, someone who was not only a great footballer but who also had a lot of time for those around him. Having been at Manchester United for so long and been part of some of their biggest success stories, it couldn't have been easy for him to leave the club he had called home for twelve years. But as well as his teammates, coaching staff and the fans, Rio also had to say goodbye to some of the people who are at the heart of every football club.

'Saying goodbye to the people at the training ground was very emotional,' he explains. 'I spent more time with some of the people at the training ground – the cleaners, dinner ladies, chefs – than I did with my own family. Going in there when nobody was training and seeing all of those people makes you realise there's more to a football club than just going out and playing.'

His move to Queens Park Rangers signalled the last phase in what had been a tremendous career, and it brought him closer to the day when he eventually decided to hang up his boots and move on to new things. So how would he like to be remembered for all those years during which he was such a fixture in the Premier League?

'When I signed for United I remember saying that if I could finish my time at Old Trafford with my head held high and had added something to the club's history I would be happy. I think I did that, and as far as my career as a professional is concerned I just want people to remember me as a player who played with passion and was good at what I did.'

LIKE RIO, STEVEN GERRARD is a player who has seen all the changes that have occurred in the Premier League, while at the same time earning a place at the top of the ladder in terms of those who have consistently performed at an incredibly high standard within the league. He is also part of a rare club, in that he is one of the few players who played week in, week out for the same Premier League club for almost seventeen years, and I don't think that sort of thing will happen too many times, if at all, in the future. Although he went off to play for LA Galaxy in the summer of 2015,

Steven was essentially a one-club man in an era when most of the top players spend their careers playing for a number of clubs in England and abroad.

He ended his Premier League career at Liverpool, having made more than 500 appearances for them. He was part of Liverpool teams that won the Champions League, two FA Cups, three League Cups and the UEFA Cup, and he also made 114 appearances in an England shirt. He became captain for Liverpool and for his country, and truly earned legendary status within the English game.

Over the years Liverpool produced some great teams, and when I played against them in the 1970s and 1980s they were the top team in England. I believe that Steven Gerrard would have been good enough to have played in any of the club's great teams. He was an exceptional player for them – he had a great engine, and the skill and ability to win a game for his side with a piece of inspirational magic, whether it was a pass or a goal. He became their talisman, and Liverpool were lucky to have him playing for them for such a long period of time. But when I talked to him it also became obvious that he feels lucky to have been able to play for them. As far as he's concerned it allowed him to live the dream of being a football-mad kid who went on to have a long career with the club he loved. He was a fan first and foremost, and it's something he has never forgotten and which played a big part in his career.

I don't think anyone who watched Steven play for Liverpool would deny that there was always a special connection between him and the supporters whenever he stepped onto the pitch. I wondered whether that sort of connection between player and supporter will continue in the years to come, or if it will soon be a thing of the past simply because there won't be the sort of home-grown talent who will stick around long enough at Liverpool – or any other Premier League club – for that sort of relationship to be built up.

'I think I was lucky,' he says. 'I was at Liverpool since I was eight, and I got the bus to watch games and stood on the Kop as a fan. So when I became a player I sort of understood the fan's side of it – why they go to the games, how hard it is for them to get to the game and what it costs. I understood all that, being a local lad. I'd seen my family do it. I'd seen my dad go and do a job just so that my brother could go and watch a game at the weekend. So I understand everyone else's situations are similar to that. That's why when I went out and played – I knew what I was playing for, what it meant to the people when we won. That's how I always tried to approach every single game as a Premier League player. There's always a circus around the matches, but I always just focused on the game and what it meant to the people who were paying to watch it.

'I think the connection can keep going, but I also think that it's important that we keep producing the players,' he insists. 'The city [of Liverpool] is known for producing good footballers, and I've watched a lot of academy games at Liverpool and Everton, and the standard is still very strong. I think the kids will come through, but I also think that the big difference between my time and now is there are so many things out there for them – there's so much money. Agents are in the players' ears now. They get agents at twelve, thirteen, fourteen years of age. I think you still get the odd player who is still a huge football fan, a one-club man, but I think it's rarer than it used to be. I think a lot more kids now are coming into the game for the rewards and what comes with it, rather than the actual love of the game or the passion for the club. The rewards now are so big, so early.

'I think a kid of seventeen or eighteen today might have the option of seven or eight different clubs who might want to give him more money than the club he's at. His agent might be making some money out of it, his parents will be making money out of it and he'll be given the wrong advice from certain people.

'In my own case I had Steve Heighway at Liverpool and my dad, all the way from eight until the age of sixteen. I had the option to go to other clubs, but there really was no financial gain at the time, plus my love was Liverpool. A lot of kids grow up and they don't really have one club. They support more than one club, and these days they might even be a Real Madrid fan, or a Messi or Ronaldo fan.'

I can completely understand what Steven means, and that's why, even in this day and age, a home-grown player who sticks with the club he loves holds a special place in the fan's affections.

'Of course I understand that,' he says. 'I also learnt from a lot of the foreign players that when they came to Liverpool they had respect for it. They knew it was a big club and how lucky they were to be here, but I also realised that for some good players and top players Liverpool was a stepping stone for them. I saw it with Mascherano, I saw it with Torres and more recently I saw it with Suárez. I think the fans appreciate the loyalty of local lads who stay with a club.

'There can be the chance to move to other clubs and there may be the chance to earn a lot of money. A lot of people ask me about Chelsea when there was talk of me going there. I've been asked why I didn't go to Chelsea – people have said I could have won a few more things, and that probably turned out to be right. The last conversation I had with my dad he said, "You win two or three medals with Liverpool and you win nine with Chelsea. Which medals will mean the most to you? Which medals will mean the most to me?" I wouldn't change my decision for anything. A lot of people are turned by things like that. Each person has their own decisions to make. For me, I never really thought about money when I was making the decision. I thought, "What's going to make me happy?" I thought about my quality of life, what was going to make my family happy and what was going to make the people who had got me to that point happy?

'There's no two ways about it, Chelsea are a quality club. I would have had a good time there, but I also knew I had it good at Liverpool. I was very well paid, I had a very good support network. I didn't want to waste it all. The connection I had with the fans. I didn't want to waste it for the sake of two or three years at a different club, or two, three, four million quid extra.

'I think things like testimonials will become very rare, because the top players will move on. They will see it as an opportunity to get richer, to have a different life experience and to get closer to where they're more comfortable. I think there's more chance of longevity with a local lad, because I think that the local people who support the club can feel that connection. I think the money side of it is a bonus. It's more about playing in front of the supporters and being a local hero. That was always my dream.

'If someone said to me now, "What was the best period of your career?" I would say – with the exception of the year we won the Champions League – it would be when I was between the ages of sixteen and eighteen. I was on £47 or £57 a week. I was doing all sorts of jobs around the first team and the banter was great. I was with my heroes, but the other thing about that time was the fact that I didn't have the pressure every single week that I later had. As a kid of that age you were enjoying your football, you weren't going out in front of 50,000 people thinking, "I've *got* to play well, we've *got* to win." It becomes a huge pressure once you've got into the first team. I think you realise once you're in it that it's different to how you thought it would be.

'Don't get me wrong. To me it's the best job in the world because I love football, but when it's your dream and you're young, you kind of only see the highlights. You see the games on TV, the goals, the celebrations, the wins, the cup finals, the trophies. You see the team – who are your heroes – doing all of this, and it becomes your dream to be part of it. Then, when you get into the first team, it becomes a pressure, because you've got to perform every single day. You've got to work hard every day, you've got to accept the criticism. The demand of being a player on a daily basis is huge. I'm not saying that it isn't what it's cracked up to be, but you realise when you get into the first-team setup that every day there is a big demand.'

Steven quite clearly took his responsibilities as a player very seriously, and it was clear from talking to him that he also took his responsibilities as the club's captain equally seriously. He lived his playing life at Anfield with certain values and with the sort of attitude that any manager would love, but I'm convinced that the game has changed in some respects when it comes to the younger players who are now trying to make it as professionals, and as captain he obviously had to deal with all sorts of personalities and situations. Different players have different ways of captaining a side and of dealing with their fellow players, so it was interesting to get a glimpse of how he dealt with matters when he was the Liverpool skipper. What did he think of some of the younger players trying to make it in the game and the way he went about the captaincy?

'Some kids would train with us and I could see they didn't have the hunger I had when I was trying to break through into the first team,' he says. 'I'm not saying I was the only one who had that hunger. There were other players. Players like the Carraghers and the Owens, where every single training session I could see it in their eyes. I could see what they wanted. Now, I think players get too much too soon.

'Some young players – not all of them – still have that hunger that we had, they still have the same motivation and dreams as I had and a lot of other players had, but more and more I see players coming into the game and wanting that path to the first team for other reasons. They see what footballers get, see the rewards, and rather than wanting it for the right reasons – the buzz of winning trophies and the buzz of playing at the top, trying to be a better player – they are in it for the rewards. For me, having the right support network is key, whether you're eight, ten or twelve, all the way up to being a thirty-five-year-old and playing at the top level. For me to make a success of my career, having the right family and friends around me and the right people at the football club was important. The wrong agents, the wrong mates or a few wrong people at a club can kill a player.

'When I was captain I saw it as one of my roles to have a word with some of the younger players if I felt that was the right thing to do, because I think once you're fifteen or sixteen and you become flash and you want football for the wrong reasons, it's too late. I think it's got to be drilled into you from an early age about the values and what football is really about. Everything else takes care of itself. The money will come, the nice cars will come. Everything will come if you do the right things as a young footballer.

'The buzz of being a professional in the first team is great. It's different when you are a professional. It's different from playing a reserve match or an 'A' team match at the training ground in front of 100 people. In the first team you're going into a dressing room with clear instructions on how to win the game. You've got thousands of people in the stadium, millions of people around the world, so it's a lot more serious. There's a lot more pressure. Being a professional at the top is not a completely enjoyable ride – it's basically ups and downs, highs and lows, and you've got to be able to deal with them both and move on very quickly.

'When you're in an environment where you've got a lot of young people, being captain of the club is a very important role because they look to see how you behave, off the pitch and on the pitch, they listen to a lot of your conversations and they want to ask you a lot of questions. I think it's more of a role-model thing, but I don't think being captain carried any greater importance than it had done previously. Whoever had been my captain in the past, I always tried to watch them. I loved being captain, I love responsibility. I'm not scared to fail, whether it be taking a penalty or having a nightmare on the pitch. I'm not scared to lose and I'm not scared of criticism. I don't like it, but I've had plenty of it and I've also had plenty of pats on the back over the years. I've done some great things on the pitch, but at the same time I know that football's not about ups and ups. It's a roller coaster. For me it's about experiences, good and bad, and come the end of it you live with them for the rest of your life. I think if players understand that it will help them an awful lot.

'When I was captain I didn't really nail people in front of other players. It was very rare. It depends on the person involved. There was a player a while ago who wasn't getting into the 1st XI, or he'd travel and wasn't in the 18 for the match and started kicking people in training. I knew he was a good person, but I felt as if it might be better to nail him in front of people. I knew he could take it, so that's why I did it. So I gave him a little bit in front of the players. He took it on board and we spoke one on one after it. I'm not taking any credit, but it helped him an awful lot. There are certain characters in a dressing room that if you did that to them it would have the opposite effect and they'd never speak to you again.

'I would say that I tried to be a captain more by example. If I saw something I didn't like I'd rather pull someone away from people and chat to them. I wasn't one of those vocal, in-your-face types, because I've worked with players and played with players who've done it to me and I didn't like it. I've been caned in front of first-team players and it's not nice. I always tried to do the right things from when I went in in the morning until I left, whether it was on the pitch or in the canteen. Things like taking your plate after you've eaten. I didn't get everything right – we all make mistakes and we're all human. But I think that once you get the role of captain you have to make huge sacrifices. You have to make sure that more often than not you're consistent, other-wise you're not doing the job properly.'

People often think players have things easy. They don't. The top ones get very well paid, but although the money is great and it enables them to enjoy a tremendous lifestyle, they also have to deal with a lot of pressure both from the need to perform on a consistent basis in training and in matches, and also from external pressure. There's no real hiding place for them, and when they reach the top they very quickly become public property. Of course they are lucky to be at the summit of their sport reaping all the rewards that go with it, but it certainly isn't one big party with everything in their lives going well.

Steven was Liverpool's talisman, digging them out of holes on many occasions, and when the team was in need of a bit of inspiration it seemed as though it was him they always looked to. That's some pressure for any player to have to deal with, even someone as talented and accomplished as him. He also had to deal with making a decision about leaving the club he loved and moving to play in a very different environment in California.

'I've felt the pressure at times,' he admits. 'I've played within myself sometimes when I've put too much pressure on myself, and I've made mistakes at times when I've put too much pressure on myself, so of course I've felt that pressure. But it was what I'd strived for, what I'd wanted since I was six or seven years of age. When I got the chance to first do it, the feeling I got was that of having a dream come true. That was the emotional side to leaving the club as a player and its captain when I went to the States, but when I went I did so knowing it was a big change for me. I didn't want to stay at Liverpool and be a sub or a squad player. I didn't want the supporters to see me as the player I hadn't been for the previous twelve years. Maybe I could have stretched it out for one more year, but I think the time was right for me to try something different.

'Whether it was going to be a complete retirement or moving on to another club, I always knew it was going to be really tough for me, because I lived the dream of playing for the club I loved. But you have to accept it. I was almost thirty-five years old when I left Liverpool as a player, and I knew I wasn't the same player as I was when I was twenty-five or twenty-six, bursting with energy, thinking that whenever I went on the pitch I could match it and mix it with anyone. It wasn't like that any more. I couldn't make ten runs into the box, I could maybe make six or seven. 'But you get signs or signals when you say to yourself, "When is the time?" Because I always felt that I was playing for the supporters, I didn't want to let them down. I didn't want them to see me getting a bit slower.

'When I dropped off for a time and stopped making the bursts I missed it, but I still enjoyed it because I had Suárez and Sturridge making runs for me. They made me get assists, but it had the opposite effect when Suárez left and Sturridge got injured. We had no pace there and teams were taking the ball off me.'

Steven was honest enough with himself to know when the time was right for him to move on. I could never imagine him playing for another club in the Premier League, and clearly the idea of moving to the States and experiencing a different way of life – while at the same time continuing his playing career at a level that wasn't quite so intense and pressurised – appealed to him. There are some very good players in the MLS, but nobody involved is kidding themselves that it compares to the sort of level he has been used to throughout his career in England.

'I'd done a long time at Liverpool and I started saying to myself that maybe I should try something different,' he concedes. 'Go and try a different lifestyle. Playing for Liverpool was fantastic, but at times it could be a difficult city to live in. You've got Liverpool and Everton. When it's not going well you can't disappear. So every day, whether you're in a coffee shop or a restaurant, you'll have a Liverpool fan saying, "That was good last night" or "Why didn't you do this or that?" and you're thinking, "Just let me finish my meal." Then you get an Everton fan who wants to throw a bottle at your car! It's a passionate city when it comes to football.

'I wanted to go to America and win games and show the sort of passion I've always done as a player, but I also knew it would be nice to go for a walk in the park, go for a coffee or go for a meal without that sort of constant attention. I lived with it for a long time, and I thought I had to be fair to my family and have a little break from it before coming back.

'But I'll still always see myself as a one-club man, because when I left I'd done twenty-six years at Liverpool. When I came back from America I wanted to go and watch Liverpool, watch the games, and I also want to try to get myself in a position where I can get another job with the club. I'm doing my coaching badges. I don't know if I'm going to be good enough to be a coach or a manager. I'd like to get to a position where I could come back and represent the club again, because I've done it for such a big part of my life. I've been asked so often whether I'm going to go into coaching or management, and the simple answer from me is, "If I'm good enough." Just because you've had a successful career as a player doesn't automatically mean the same will be the case as a coach or manager.

'Hopefully I'll get the opportunity at Liverpool to get some experience, and I also think it will be important to go to different places and sit down with different managers at different clubs, to see how they work, to try to learn. But I'm miles away from that at the moment.'

LIKE STEVEN GERRARD, there is no doubt at all that Frank Lampard was one of the most consistent performers the Premier League has ever had. His quality, ability and professionalism shone through whenever he stepped onto the pitch, and it is no coincidence that he had such a long and distinguished career at the top. Frank worked his socks off to achieve what he did as a player, using every ounce of ability he had to become one of the Premier League's greats.

I have known him since he was a kid, because his dad, Frank senior, played for West Ham when I first started my career as a youngster. He was a full-back and a dedicated professional, who would often put in extra work on the training ground. He was as hard as nails as a player, and wingers knew they'd been tackled when they came up against him. He also used to take training sessions with some of the young schoolboy players the club had, and I was one of the kids who was coached by him. Frank was great with me and would often give me a lift back home because his parents lived just around the corner from me. His work ethic as a player clearly rubbed off on his son. It seems that his influence played a major part in making sure young Frank would follow in his dad's footsteps and become a professional footballer by making the most of his talents and constantly working to improve his game.

'It was probably 99 per cent down to my dad,' admits Frank. 'He'd been that sort of player. He was short of genuine pace and was obsessed with speed. He imprinted that on me. Even as a kid of ten years of age I'd be told about going with runners and doing all the nasty stuff that you don't really want to do. Not the sort of thing a ten-year-old would normally be doing, but it was real basics and it gave me a proper football knowledge. He was quite intense, and he was also one of those sorts who would always talk about the pitfalls that went with the game – typical old school! He'd tell you what could go wrong instead of all the great stuff that might be associated with being a footballer. But looking back now, I think it was brilliant, because as a kid you need that grounding. I think I grew up aware of my weaknesses and what I didn't have in my game. So I became obsessed by his obsessions. Things like speed, running and agility.

'I think he thought I lacked a bit of pace, and he was probably right. I was a sort of chubby kid at certain times in my development, so I think agility was maybe a bit of a problem – getting around the pitch. I think he basically relived a lot of what he'd done himself through me. He could see I needed to do it as well, and in the end it became a part of me. As a kid I didn't really want to do it. All I wanted to do was enjoy my football, and doing sprints on a rainy day when you're fifteen is not enjoyable when all you want to do is hit shots at goal. I don't want to make it sound as if he was a complete taskmaster, because he wasn't, but those extra bits helped. My dad always talks about the extra 10 per cent or the extra 20 per cent. He wanted to give me that extra 20 per cent, which was all the nasty stuff, but he knew it would help and it did.

'During my career I associated all the nasty stuff on the training ground during the week with me being successful. Things like hitting loads of shots could end up with me scoring a goal with a deflection at the weekend. So you end up living your life in a bit of an OCD type of way. If I didn't do my sprints in midweek I didn't feel I was going to have a good game at the weekend. It was something I've carried on right through my career, and it's probably only slowed down in recent years, probably because your body is telling you that you can't carry on in quite the same way.

'I remember that when I went from West Ham to Chelsea in 2001 the fitness coach didn't like me doing some of the extra things I'd always been used to doing, like extra runs in spikes. It was something my dad made me do, and his thinking was that it would help make me lighter on my feet rather than heavy footed – and it did help me. But when I got to Chelsea the fitness coach wouldn't let me do the spikes, saying it would be bad for me. So I used to hide them and do the runs over the back of the training ground in a corner! It almost didn't matter how many I did. Even if it was only five or six it was just about putting them on and doing it – the OCD thing.

'When you do make it at a club like Chelsea they probably trust you more. So sometimes, the day after a game, even if I'd gone out for a couple of beers I'd go in and do a twenty-minute run. The fitness coach would say that scientifically it wasn't very good for me, but I'd do it anyway. You learn when it's best to do the extra work. I remember towards the end of José Mourinho's first spell at the club I did extra sprints on a Thursday after the training session had finished and ended up pulling my thigh. I did get a bit of a bollocking for that, but looking back now he was really all right about it. I think he knew why I'd done it and what it was about. But I was out for six weeks, and you learn when you should and shouldn't do certain stuff. Doing that at the end of a training session when your body's tired means you might get pulls, so I adjusted the extra stuff I did along the way and worked with my managers. I remember Claudio Ranieri wouldn't want you doing extra shooting after training. My shooting near a weekend was a massive thing for me, but I sometimes had to swallow it and not do it.'

Frank has always been known for being an intelligent footballer who knew how to read the game, but he was also an intelligent boy at school, gaining eleven GCSEs before starting his career at West Ham. Although it was clear at a fairly young age that he had what it takes to be a footballer, things were not always easy for him. At the time the club was managed by Harry Redknapp, who just happened to be young Frank's uncle, and his dad was Harry's assistant. He had to put up with 'teacher's pet' jibes even though he made it into the first team on merit. He had an insight into what it was like to be a professional footballer having been brought up with a dad who was one, but because of that it didn't follow that he would make it. Frank never took anything for granted – that wasn't the way he was brought up. He knew that if he was going to succeed he would have to work just as hard as his dad had, and he certainly never got anything handed to him on a plate.

'I always wanted to be a footballer, but I always had a huge fear of not making it,' he says. 'Like most kids I dreamed about it, but because of my dad I was probably less naïve than other kids. If I had a good game I never got carried away with what I'd done, because my dad would bring me back down to earth. I never just assumed I would make it. I did all right at school because I was quite conscientious – I revised well, I wanted to please my teachers, I wanted to please my parents. I was that sort of kid. I also think now that it was a great fallback for me had I not made it as a footballer. That was what I always wanted to be, although I did think about maybe being a lawyer at one time, but that was probably more to do with the fact that I used to watch *L.A. Law* on television! But being a footballer was really what I wanted, and I was happy that I eventually made it.

'I did find it difficult at times when I was at West Ham because of the connection with my dad. Even in my Sunday team I was always "Lampard's son", because he was quite well known in the area, so you would get other parents and other kids wanting to get one over on you. When I did sign for West Ham it was a bit messy at times because fans and people around the club thought I was getting a head start.

I'm not going to lie – I found it tough, from when I first signed for them to when I left there. To be honest I felt slightly bitter when I left, because having to live with that whole thing bugged me a lot. It wasn't nice, and I'd go home really upset with it. When I warmed up at the side of the pitch during a game you'd hear people telling me to go and sit down with my old man. Some of my family would tell me about stuff they'd heard, and I didn't take it well. Looking back, it's easy to say it was character building, but the truth is that at the time it was difficult. At one stage I actually thought, "Am I better off dropping down a league?" just to get away from the intensity of it all. When I did leave the club I felt quite bitter for a good few years. That period was a tough thing for me.'

Frank eventually left the club in the summer of 2001, moving to Chelsea for £11 million. His father and Harry Redknapp had already left West Ham a few months earlier, and as well as Chelsea both Leeds and Aston Villa were keen to sign him.

'My eyes were on leaving before the two of them went,' he says, 'but my dad going was a catalyst for me. I went up to Leeds and sat with David O'Leary, who was their manager at the time. He said he wanted to buy me, but he was signing Seth Johnson as well and I'd have to fight for my place, so I came away from the meeting thinking he hadn't really sold it to me brilliantly. Villa were also interested but I didn't really fancy going there, and then Chelsea came out of nowhere. They had some good players there, people like Jimmy Floyd Hasselbaink and Marcel Desailly. Ken Bates was the chairman, and he was brilliant. I know some people say negative things about him, but for me he was brilliant. He paid the money for me and took me to the club. He was a larger-than-life character. When I spoke to the manager, Claudio Ranieri, he said he was going to buy Emmanuel Petit – he wanted me in midfield with him, Bolo Zenden on the left and Mario Stanic on the right, and I thought, "That'll do for me!" There was a clear picture of what he wanted. They were a top six, or top eight club at the time, but I never thought things would take off in the way they did. That all happened when Roman Abramovich came in and bought Chelsea two years after I went there.

'I remember that in that second season I was there the club had real money problems. We were all told that we needed to get into the Champions League otherwise that could be it, we were probably going bust. We did on the last day of the season, and a couple of months later Abramovich came in and bought the club. We had a terrible training ground at the time in Harlington, and on Wednesdays we used to get thrown out to make way for a university team to come and play there. So you had someone like Desailly, who'd won a World Cup winner's medal with France a few years earlier, having to get changed quickly to let a university kid with his socks around his ankles come in! At that time Chelsea were a mixture of a club that had a great stadium, good players and a terrible training ground. Soon after he bought it, Abramovich landed at Harlington in his helicopter. He looked around and then said something to the bloke standing next to him. This guy was his translator, and it turned out that what he said was, "I'm getting rid of this shithole." That was the start of it, and things really began to take off in a way I couldn't really have imagined when I first signed for them.'

One of the most impressive aspects of Frank's game over the years has been his ability to get into the box, arriving at just the right time to connect with the ball and have a shot on goal. I've lost count of the number of times he did this during his time in the Premier League, and despite the fact that players knew all about the threat he posed, more often than not he was still able to make those runs, get his shot in and score goals. From the spectacular shots just outside the penalty box, to the close-range tap-ins from a few feet out, they all counted – and nobody was fully able to combat what he was able to do. He's had the ability to make a move one way, check and then move. Other players knew he would always be trying to do it, but there were many times when he just wasn't picked up because he'd lost them. So when did he discover that he had that knack of being able to ghost into the box?

'I think it was something that evolved,' he says. 'In my youth-team days my dad said to me that if I wanted to be a midfielder who made a name for himself, then I had to score goals. He said that I had to try to be quicker and fitter, so I worked on that and scored quite a few goals in the youth team, and I also scored for West Ham when I got in the first team. But at that point I think I just used to get in the box and sort of wait for something to happen. My dad used to dig me out and say, "You went into the box and just waited.

You've got to go in and then come out again and then go in."
So I started to do that, but when I went to Chelsea Ranieri
was on at me about discipline in midfield, so I stopped
making those sort of runs and started playing in the middle
of the park. It wasn't a bad thing, because I was getting
involved with play and learning about keeping possession,
but in my first couple of seasons I scored single figures.

'But in the third season there were new players coming in
and I thought, "I've got to do a bit more here." The quality
of the team rose, and if you did make a run you'd get a
better ball. And that's when it really started. I think I got
fifteen goals that season, then it was nineteen, and then
twenty, twenty-one, twenty, twenty and in 2010 it was twenty-seven. I think it was a confidence thing as well. I also
learnt that midfielders hate running back with you. I hate it
as well, we all do, but that's the dirty side of the game. I used
to score loads of goals in the second half of a game when
they didn't want to run and they're knackered. I also learned
about running on the angle. Centre-halves didn't get you if
you stayed on the move, and you always have to expect
things, for the ball to get to you. In the early days I would
think a lot more about what I had to do, and then in the
middle part of my career I suppose I was on autopilot and
you don't have to think as much. But then when you get
older you have to start thinking about it again and pushing
yourself to do the right things – going in, checking out,
making the runs.

'You have to make sure you're fit enough to get into the
box and cute enough with your play to make room for

yourself. You've got to do the leg work and you have to practise. I used to practise at Chelsea loads, receiving the ball from the left-winger or left-midfielder, getting it out of my feet quickly and then having a shot. I've scored loads of goals like that. Some have gone straight in and some have taken a deflection and gone in, but they all counted. It's great scoring from twenty yards out, but it's also good being in the right place three yards out and getting the tap-ins. But I could never have done it without putting in the leg work, and I always thought that if I was fitter than the other bloke I was already 1–0 up in our personal battle in a game.'

Frank is of a generation that has seen a lot of changes in the Premier League and the way it has evolved, and, like Rio and Steven, he was able to maintain a consistent level of performance at the top, something that separates all the great players from the rest. He was also able to maintain his place in a Chelsea team that regularly had world stars added to the squad. After being signed by Ranieri, Frank went on to play under a further eight managers, all of whom recognised the qualities he brought to the team. It's probably fair to say that his Chelsea career really began to take off and flourish under José Mourinho, when he first arrived at Stamford Bridge in 2004.

'There's no doubt he had an effect on the team and an effect on me,' he admits. 'It wasn't anything tactical, it was just his way – the bravado and self-confidence he showed. He said to me, "You're a great player, a great midfielder, you're the best." I knew I wasn't the best but I still thought,

"Hang on a minute, I'd better do something here." I reacted to it and knew that I had to be good. He expected certain things from his players, and I couldn't afford to be rubbish. His thoughts about me and what he wanted were sort of imprinted on me from that moment.

'Things certainly changed once he arrived, but the game in the Premier League is constantly changing and I think things definitely moved on from when I first played in it. I think physically the game has moved on a lot, and the speed of the football. I think there was a different mindset off the pitch as well when I first started. I think a quality player from those early days of my career would still be a quality player now, but the pace has gone up a notch or two and tactically I think we're more aware now. I also think the influx of foreign players and managers at the top end of the game has helped the quality of the league. The culture is different now with regard to young players, but I would say that those that get to the top handle themselves better with things like nutrition, lifestyle and training. But it's different now for kids – I went out on loan to Swansea when I was at West Ham and then got in the team when I was seventeen. At Chelsea now you've got no chance unless you're Messi or top, top end as a player. So young players can end up sitting around for two or three years and their attitude can go a bit. It's very difficult.

'Things were different when I started. We'd play youth games on the Saturday morning, get in a minibus back to Upton Park, with a stop at McDonald's on the way back, watch the game, then stand in the tunnel as the first team came off the pitch before cleaning up the dressing rooms after they'd finished with them. We hated it at times, but looking back now I can see what a brilliant grounding it was. Now kids get two tickets for a game and some of them give them away to their mates – they don't even watch the match! We had to. Not all of them do it, but it shows how different things are now.

'It's tough now for the youngsters to come through at big clubs. The great ones will always come through, but if you take someone like me, there's no way I'd have got into Chelsea's first team if it was now. When I was seventeen, eighteen, nineteen or twenty I wouldn't have got past the likes of Matic and Fàbregas, and then would I have developed in the way that I did? I would have ended up falling by the wayside.

'I think if good kids are going to come through you need a good first-team manager who links in, bringing you through as a youngster – if you're good enough – to train with the first team. Make you feel like you're part of the squad and talk to you. There were times when I was at Chelsea where certain managers didn't link youngsters in. When I was young and at West Ham, if the first-team squad was one short in training, Harry Redknapp would make a point of bringing you over to train with them. These days some managers don't care if they're one short – they just get on and train with what they've got. At Chelsea in the last two or three years that I was there we had a bit of a process going on where if there was a young centre-half doing well he would go and speak to John Terry. John would look at videos of them playing in games and talk to them about playing centre-half, and I did the same with some of the promising midfielders. The more you do it, the more you realise that they do take a lot from it and they're pleased that you took the time to talk to them. I think there's a massive responsibility at any club to keep the boys involved and make them feel part of it all.'

As with Rio and Steven, Frank knows what it is like to live in the sort of spotlight that comes with being a top professional footballer in the Premier League. I can't help feeling that his background and the down-to-earth values his dad instilled in him at a very young age must have helped him during his career. The way he has worked and continues to work at his game is an example to any young player who wants to make it to the very top. He has won three Premier League titles, four FA Cups, two League Cups and the Champions League, as well as making 106 appearances for England and captaining his country. But he has never once been the sort of person to sit back and take things easy. Last year saw him begin a new chapter in his playing career when he went to the States and played for New York City. He's realistic and honest enough to know that retirement as a player is now on the horizon for him, but he clearly intends to keep his options open when it come to the day he will eventually hang up his boots, and he's enjoyed the challenge of playing in the States.

'I think you learn to cope with the spotlight thing,' he says. 'I'm lucky because the area of London I live in is quite cosmopolitan. I'm quite a shy boy, not a real people person or someone who will go out and say, "Here I am!" But let's get it right. It's brilliant the way the game's gone and everyone's done pretty well out of it. The finances have changed so much and the Premier League is a worldwide brand – and you have to embrace that. I still think I'm pretty lucky with the way people treat me. In Italy, as a player, you could be having dinner and someone will grab you. That doesn't happen here. It can be hard sometimes, but I never want to give the wrong impression. I've got two girls and they love One Direction. If they saw Harry Styles from the group and he blanked them, I'd half get the hump with him! But I can understand the fact that he could have had his picture taken a 100 times with fans that day and he might just want a rest from it.

'As for going to New York it was something I wanted to do, going to play abroad. I flirted with the idea earlier in my career, going to Italy and Milan when Mourinho was at Inter. I always wanted to take on a bit of a challenge, and when I left Chelsea it was perfect. The spell with Manchester City, which I enjoyed, came along in the interim, but going to play in New York excited me. I'm quite a home boy, so going there was a bit of a challenge, but it was a good challenge for me – doing something different – and I've enjoyed it.

'As for what will happen when I do stop playing, I don't really know. I'd like to do my coaching badges, but I'm not sure I want to be a manager. I feel that I've had a really long career and I've got quite a few other interests. I maybe wouldn't mind working in football behind the scenes.

Obviously having the financial security is nice, but whenever I do finish I would like to do something. What's the point of getting out of bed to sit there and reflect on a career? But when the day comes I think I'll be ready for it. I'm not one of those players who will miss the dressing room. Don't get me wrong. I've got good friends in football, but I'm not someone who has to rely on my mates in the dressing room to have a laugh and a joke every day. I like that side of it, but I don't need the constant lads' banter. I can have a different sort of lifestyle that maybe isn't so rigid.

'I'll be able to wake up in the morning and think about what I want to do.'

CHAPTER 4

RETIREMENT

Jamie Carragher, Ryan Giggs

WHEN FOOTBALLERS RETIRE they have to make some significant choices about the next phase of their lives and, unless they have a very clear picture of what they are going to do, it can be extremely hard for some of them to adjust to life after playing. There have been many cases of players finding it difficult to cope with retirement and becoming depressed as the routines they have known for twenty years and more are no longer part of their lives. They miss the buzz of playing in front of thousands of people each week, the elation they got from winning matches and even the emptiness of a defeat. They miss the daily training and the banter of the dressing room, they miss their teammates and they miss that touch of glory that comes with being part of a team when you win.

When you are playing professional football there can be a tendency to only think short term and to believe that your career will go on and on. Players battle and work hard to become professionals and most have dreamed of nothing else since they were kids. But once they retire, the ordered and structured way of life they have become used to is no longer there. Suddenly they don't have to get up for training in the morning, and if they don't have something meaningful to fill their lives there can be a problem. Of course, it helps if you have millions in the bank and are financially secure for life, because the need to go out and earn money doesn't exist in the same way that it might do for someone who has spent their career in the lower leagues. But it is that feeling of worth, of doing something with your life that has a purpose, that retired footballers from all levels of the game have to learn to cope with and plan for.

In my own case I felt that I wanted to continue in the game when I finished playing, but I was lucky in many ways. I never had to deal with that moment when one day you are a player and the next day you are not, or when a manager calls you in and says he's not going to be offering you another contract and that it might be time for you to pack in playing. In the latter part of my playing career I was already helping out with some coaching at Charlton, who at that time were struggling financially and didn't even have a ground of their own. They had been sharing Selhurst Park with Crystal Palace and were about to end that arrangement and move in with West Ham at Upton Park. The manager, Lennie Lawrence, then got the chance to go to Middlesbrough, and the club were left with a decision to make about who should replace him.

In the end they made what was an unusual choice by appointing me and another player-coach, Steve Gritt, as joint player-managers. We were thrown in at the deep end and had to do everything. It was a great learning curve for both of us, and although I continued as a player as well for a while, the managerial side of things meant that my days on the pitch were limited and in the end came to a natural end. Then in 1995, four years after I took over with Steve, the club decided they wanted me to take sole charge and become manager. So I never really had to sit down and plan for the end of my career – things just seemed to move from one phase to another. Even though it was really tough in those early days with Steve at Charlton, we enjoyed it and it gave me tremendous experience, which I know helped me later in my career as a manager. I also felt as a player that I wanted to stay in the game and coach or manage, so that was in my mind. Had it not been Charlton, I would have tried my luck somewhere else in the hope of making the progression from player to coach to manager.

YOU OFTEN HEAR people in the game talking about certain players and saying that they think they will become a coach or manager. It's usually the sort of player who has always been interested in tactics and formations, someone who takes an interest in the way training sessions are put on, who likes going out and watching matches, and who will often be asking the manager all sorts of questions. A player like Jamie Carragher, for instance, would have ticked all those boxes. He was a tremendous defender, a great reader of the game and someone who clearly thought about football and the way teams played. You could tell he had a real passion for football and it wouldn't have surprised me in the least if Jamie had decided to move into coaching and management when he retired as a player in 2013.

Instead he began a new career in the media, more specifically as a pundit with Sky and a newspaper columnist with the *Daily Mail*. His analysis alongside Gary Neville on Sky's *Monday Night Football* programme was instantly popular when they were teamed together. They did a great job of giving the viewer a real insight into what had gone on in various matches over the weekend and neither of them were afraid to give their views and opinions of teams, managers and players. Gary left in December 2015 to take over at Valencia as their manager, and I'm sure that if Jamie had wanted to move into coaching or management instead of the media nobody would have been surprised. It would have seemed like the logical next step for someone like him, so why did he choose a television studio instead of a training pitch?

'There were two managers at Liverpool during my time as a player with the club who had the biggest influence on my career,' says Jamie. 'Gérard Houllier and Rafa Benítez. I had them for six years each, but to be honest, seeing them do the job put me off management!

'When I was in my mid-twenties I was 100 per cent going to be a manager. I would be writing things down, writing squads down – who I'd buy, who I'd sell from Liverpool's point of view. In the end, under Benítez, I was getting training-session plans and all sorts of things. In the first three or four years that each of them were at the club they were getting so much respect, but then when it turned the other way and results went against them, you could see the effect it had on them. You started to think, "This isn't the same person." They're different, and you almost sort of feel sorry for them. The paranoia kicks in a little bit, and you see them having strange press conferences or you read strange quotes in the papers. I always say when I talk about the two of them that the man who walked in to the club wasn't the same as the man who walked out. You look at them both and think about the effect it had on each of them. So it makes you think about the whole thing.

'When I knew I was getting towards the end of my career I told the club. I told Brendan Rodgers the first time I met him after he took over as manager. I said that I had a year to go and that I was retiring at the end of that. When Kenny Dalglish was finishing towards the end of the season in 2012 before Brendan took over, I'd asked if the following pre-season I could sort of shadow him. Sit in on meetings and get a little flavour of what it was all like. But the other thing I did that summer was the Euros for ITV, and I enjoyed it, mixing with the other lads and watching the games. I think Sky also saw what I did that summer and they made contact, but it wasn't until about halfway through my last season that I decided to go to Sky.

'It wasn't as though I was waiting for Liverpool to offer me something – it was more a case of me thinking that I had to do something, and I'd told the club I was retiring so they knew. When I'd thought about the idea of shadowing Kenny, I wouldn't say I was 100 per cent sure that I wanted to be a coach or manager, but I wanted to find out more. The way I played the game, the way I was on the pitch, always talking to other players and trying to organise. I was consumed by football, but I still didn't know what coaching and management were like. People would say to me, "You could be a coach or a manager," but I'd be thinking about what it actually entailed, and until you've done it or been close to it you don't really know. So that's why I did ITV that summer. I wanted to see what that was like as well. In the end I liked it and decided to do the Sky thing when I was asked.

'When I was a player I used to read everything I could about the game and watch all the matches I could. I've always been like that. And now, what I like about the punditry is the detail I can get into. With the *Monday Night Football* show I love finding something in a game that no one else has seen, or getting into the real fine detail of something that has happened in a match. We have longer to look at things than they do on *Match of the Day*. They have to show all the games and the goals, but we can look at the matches from over the weekend and maybe focus on two big things, that's the beauty of it. Basically I think we're actually doing the sort of thing a manager might do on a Monday morning after a match, maybe looking at a ten-minute period of play where a team was 2–1 up but was unable to protect that lead and conceded a goal.'

It's obvious that Jamie takes his TV work every bit as seriously as he did his playing career when he was a footballer. He's enjoying his work in the media and the newfound freedom it has given him in terms of his lifestyle. He's at home more with his family, and although he has to travel to matches or to the Sky studios in west London, it's nothing compared to what he experienced as a player. Jamie played the game with a passion and intensity that not only demanded a lot from his teammates, but also from himself. It must have been a big decision to finally call a halt to his playing career. It must have also been a big change to his way of life, as he left behind all the routines and structure of a life he had known since he was a kid.

'I don't miss it,' he insists. 'I miss the big games, but I don't miss the training. Towards the end of my career I was getting to the stage where I wasn't playing every week. So I was training more, and it becomes a grind and you don't really look forward to it. I did get into the team for the last three or four months, but for about eighteen months previously I'd been a sub. I knew it was the right time for me to stop playing.

'When I was playing, right through my career, I was very up and down. If I made a mistake or was in a bad run of form it would affect me. I wouldn't say I'd struggle to sleep, but it would constantly be on my mind. I'd be thinking, "I've got to play well in the next game." When it came to things like the international break when I'd stopped playing for England, if Liverpool had lost going into the break I would be going over and over the game, and you had to wait two weeks before you played again. That was the way I played, and it was probably worse when I was at my best as a player.

'I got to the stage, probably between 2005 and 2009, when I was maybe playing as well as anyone in my position, and as a team we were good defensively and kept a lot of clean sheets. So I'd be thinking, "I've got to play well for us to get a result today," because I knew that in the position I played in, if I made a mistake it could mean we lost the game. I wouldn't say it affected my performance, because as a player I was probably at the best I was ever at, but it was the way I played – and it kept me on my toes. It's nice that now I've finished playing I don't have all of that.

'As a player I was always striving to do better, and being a local lad I think that when we won a trophy it meant more to people like me and Stevie Gerrard. We knew what it meant to the fans and your family. The other side of it was that when you lost it felt much worse because you felt as though you'd let people down. Liverpool's a city, but it's not a big city. Everyone knows everyone, and it's more like a village in a strange way. I love it. The people have got something about them, they're characters and there's a bit of grit. The passion for football probably matches or beats anywhere in the country, but what I like now about doing the work with Sky is that I'm out of the bubble of Liverpool Football Club. I like the fact that it's not all Liverpool, it's the Premier League.

'So now we might do a show and we might not even touch on Liverpool. Of course, I've got a season ticket at Liverpool and I still go to games, but I like the fact that Liverpool's results don't affect me in the way they did when I was a player. When I was a Liverpool player and I did an interview you're always talking about Liverpool. I love football, so now I can give my opinion of what I think is right or wrong at Manchester United or Arsenal. You'd have those opinions before, but you wouldn't be in a position to say them. Everything was Liverpool, Liverpool, Liverpool.

'I'm also at home a lot more now. As a player you couldn't even organise a night out, because if Liverpool got beat you'd say, "We're not going out!" Now I've got a bit more of a balanced life. You don't have the buzzes that you had from winning, but you don't have the downs from losing either. We get a buzz from doing the show on a Monday night, but it will never match beating Everton at Goodison or Manchester United in a final.'

I don't think any footballer can fully replace the feelings they got from winning big matches, and that's only natural, but Jamie clearly enjoys his media work. The two things that have stayed the same for both him and Gary Neville are the work ethic they brought to their careers as players and the fact that they are both naturally team players, recognising the work put in by others and the fact that you can't get the job done unless you're all pulling in the same direction.

'I don't think either Gary or me were the greatest players when it came to natural talent,' he says. 'We had to be fully focused, be professional, be switched on. We were probably like that in training every day as well. We wanted to work and give ourselves the best chance. I think that when we worked together we had the same sort of attitude. We'd both do our prep before doing the show. Be in at 9.30 on the morning it was going out and leave about 11.30 that night. It wouldn't feel right if I hadn't done all the work beforehand – it's something I've always done.

'The show itself is a huge team effort because there are so many people behind the scenes who help make it work and who you rely on. We both used to enjoy doing the television work and at the end of the show it was a bit like being a player. Back then you knew if you'd played well and had a good game, and with television you know whether things have worked, whether you've had a good show. If it's not gone right, then you look at why it didn't and make sure you work on it, because you don't want it to happen again.'

I think Jamie's approach to his media work is very similar to how he approached football. He worked hard throughout his life as a player to be the best he could be, and now he wants to do the same when a camera is pointed at him in the television studio. The move from playing to working in the media appears to have been a smooth one for him, and he has found a way of staying very much involved in the game and enjoying it without taking the coaching or management route. The media is certainly something a lot more top players are likely to try and move into in the coming years, and perhaps there won't be so many wanting to move into management, particularly as they will be financially secure for life and, like Jamie, will have seen what the stresses and strains of the job can do to a person.

* * *

SOMEONE WHO HAS had one of the best Premier League careers and won pretty much everything at club level is Ryan Giggs. During a magnificent twenty-four-year playing career that started in 1990 and ended in 2014 he made more than 670 appearances for Manchester United and is recognised as one of the greatest players ever to have worn the famous red shirt. After moving into a player-coaching role towards the end of his career, Ryan was given a taste of just what it is like to be the man in charge when he became United's interim manager for the last four games of the 2013–14 season, after David Moyes lost his job. He won two games, drew another and suffered a defeat during his brief spell as boss.

When Louis van Gaal was appointed as the new manager at Old Trafford for the start of the 2014–15 season, Ryan became his assistant and has made no secret of his ambition to become a manager in his own right at some date. But for the moment Ryan's focus is on learning a new trade within the game and equipping himself as best he can to one day go on and become a manager.

'I've been lucky because it's been like a natural progression for me,' he says. 'The circumstances were right. After Sir Alex left and David Moyes took over he asked me to be a coach, but also play as well. It was such a great chance for me to learn my trade while still playing. It was quite difficult juggling the two, but I wanted to help him as much as I could because I knew the club and he didn't. It was a win–win situation for me. He was an experienced Premier League manager and I knew it was going to be my last year. It just seemed the natural way to go for me. I know that from a lifestyle point of view going into something like TV would have meant I spent more time with my family, but I was used to going in to training every day and not having days off. I also knew that if I did want to go and do TV work at some stage, I wanted to do coaching and management first.

'David might not have been successful during his time at the club, but I learned a lot from him and the way he worked. He did some really good things, and with Louis coming in the same applies. I'm reaping the benefits of having those two managers in a short space of time, and obviously having Sir Alex as my manager for so long when I was playing, you're learning from the best.

'When you're in football you never know what is going to happen. That's why I took my coaching badges when I was playing. I wanted to be prepared as much as possible, and for me this is definitely the best way, rather than going straight into a manager's position. I've always felt that I was more manager than coach, but you need to get that experience of coaching. I needed to learn how to coach, to put on sessions and go out there and do it day in, day out. I had a clear vision about what I wanted to do. I didn't want to stop playing and think, "Right, what do I do now?" I was lucky in lots of ways because first David asked me to coach and then Louis asked me to come on board when he took over, but I definitely didn't want to stop playing and not have anything organised. It's worked well for me and I feel I'm so much more knowledgeable now when it comes to the way things work on a day-to-day basis than I was eighteen months ago.'

Although I think Ryan made the right choice to go into coaching before even thinking about the prospect of becoming a manager, he did get an invaluable taste of what it is like to be the man in charge at such a massive club as Manchester United when he had that four-game period as interim manager between David Moyes leaving and Louis van Gaal taking over. It was clearly an eye-opener for him, and he was also able to learn some important lessons for when the day finally comes when he feels ready to become a manager.

'The big thing it did teach me was to follow your instincts,' says Ryan. 'I had three home games against Norwich, Sunderland and Hull, followed by a trip to Southampton. I knew straight away when I looked at the fixtures that Sunderland was the hardest game, and yet in the end I played probably the weakest team and we lost 1–0. My speech when I first took over was, "Listen, I trust you all." Big mistake! I tried to give everyone confidence, tried to say that you're all going to get a game. We'd beaten Norwich 4–0 in my first game, so I mixed it around for the Sunderland game, although at that time Sunderland were on a roll. I felt terrible after that. I went home and my kids were talking to me, but I wasn't listening. All I could think about was the game and it was the same for a long time after it. We beat Hull and drew at Southampton, but I never think about those matches. The one I think about is losing to Sunderland and I learned more from that experience than I did from any of the other games. It's a bad feeling when you're in charge and you lose – you want to kill the players! But being in charge for that short period was a brilliant experience for me. I made loads of mistakes, but the whole thing was invaluable. You can do all the badges, but those four games were better than the whole of my pro licence.

'I'd been managed by Sir Alex for so long and obviously you pick little bits up as a player, but it's totally different being the manager. He would get in at say 6.30 in the morning and he'd be gone by 2. When I took over I thought I would just get in at a normal time, say 7.30 or 8am, but I was staying a little bit longer – and I learned a lesson from that. The longer you stay, the more people come knocking on your door and you're being pulled left, right and centre. I also had things like the young lads' contracts to deal with, because it was towards the end of the season when I was in charge. So there were so many different little things.'

As a player Ryan would have seen the way Sir Alex Ferguson operated, and that experience over such a long period of time can only be a great help when the time comes for him to venture into the world of management. But observing a manager, even one as great as Sir Alex, is still nothing like being on the other side of the fence as part of the first-team management setup at a club. So working with David Moyes and with Louis van Gaal clearly meant that Ryan was exposed to many different things that he never got involved in as a player. He also had to get used to walking onto the training pitch and putting a session on that would engage and command the respect of twenty players. It can be daunting, even for someone who has had the magnificent career he had as a player, and there are always new things to be learned, whether you have hundreds of games under your belt as a coach or manager or you are just starting out.

'You can't think as a player,' insists Ryan. 'I took a session one day and Louis was watching. It was attack vs defence. I was telling some of the midfield players what to do and at the end of the session Louis told me that what I'd said was right, but that basically I hadn't explained it as I should have done. I just thought what should be done was obvious, because it was what I would have done as a player. But my job was to explain it all to everyone in detail so that they knew what I was thinking and what I wanted them to do. I've seen Steve McClaren and René Meulensteen put on sessions when they were at United and they could get their message over every day. I don't think I could be as good as them, but I was always good with people, I was always good at decision making and I'm not bothered about upsetting anyone.

'The good thing about Louis is that he's totally transparent. He tells you everything, so you end up not having to ask questions. He also wants you to be transparent with him. He tells you how he feels – you might not like it, but he tells you – and he tells the players directly as well. I'm just trying to take everything in and sometimes I might think, "That's good," or sometimes, "I would have done it differently." But you just don't need to ask questions with Louis – he tells you everything anyway!

'I'll do things like analysis of the opposition and other people will do other things like set pieces. Louis will oversee all the meetings but he doesn't put them together. He just says things like, "No, you should take that out," or "Put this in." That's where Louis is good. His mind's quite clear when it comes to the game and the overall picture. He's overseen everything, but he's got the confidence to delegate to people he trusts, which was something Sir Alex had as well with all the coaches he had during his time at the club.

'I'm still enthusiastic about the job, but it does feel like there are more "downs" than there are "ups". It was the reverse when you were a player. I used to get down when we lost and it could ruin the weekend, but it's not the same as when you're on the management side of things. But I love the job. I love coming in, I love learning every day and I love taking the session. The thing that maybe puts you off management a little bit is the landscape. You see managers getting sacked – I don't really think about it too much, but it is something that could put you off. Your centre-forward might get injured and that could be the end of your career. It's ridiculous really, that managers don't get that much time.'

The reality of being a manager these days is that clubs expect almost instant success or they start to look elsewhere. Ryan was lucky to have someone like Sir Alex for so long, but that situation is never likely to happen again in the modern game. As soon as Ryan became part of Louis van Gaal's management setup there was talk that one day he would be the natural successor when the Dutchman eventually left Old Trafford. I certainly didn't get the impression that taking on such a big job would faze him in any way, but he is level-headed enough to know that his opportunity in management might not come with United. What he is sure about is the need to prepare himself in the best possible way so that when any opportunity comes along he is ready to take it.

'The talk about me possibly being manager at Manchester United has no effect on me. I'm just learning all the time,' he says. 'You have to be open and not so blinkered to think there's only one option. You've got to be open and you've got to prepare yourself as best you can. That's what I'm trying to do every day. You do things in the week – and then if they come off and you win it's a brilliant feeling. Nothing will ever replace playing, but I knew that. I think management is the second-best thing. Just like when you're a player you have to make sacrifices. I've got two young kids and I never see them, whereas when I was playing I'd pick them up from school every day. But that sort of thing is just something you have to deal with, and when I do spend time with them I have to make sure it's quality time. You have to manage your life as best you can, and that's what I'm seeing now. That's what Louis is good at and what Sir Alex was good at. When it comes to the big decisions they have to make, they are very clear thinking.

'What's good for me, having worked with both of them, is that I know they have their doubts about things sometimes. From the outside you're thinking, "They never doubt themselves, they're always confident," but of course they have their doubts. You could always tell with Sir Alex when we were having a big game, when Liverpool were coming up, because that nervous cough would come out! You knew that even after twenty years he was probably asking himself if he'd done everything right. I know that doubt will never leave you as a manager. It's all part of the job.'

Management is a tough job, but it can also be incredibly rewarding and fulfilling. Ryan has got to give it a go. I hope it's at Manchester United, but wherever it is and whenever it is you've got to give yourself the best possible preparation in order to succeed – and Ryan Giggs is doing just that.

CHAPTER 5

YOUTH

Jón Thorsteinsson

THERE ARE PROBABLY millions of kids around the world who dream of making it as a professional footballer. The reality is that only a tiny handful of those kids actually get to fulfil their dreams. If they do make it, they will have had to have gone through all sorts of trials and obstacles to earn their living from playing the game.

It's very easy for fans to look at players and think they have a great life just for kicking a ball about. That's true in one sense. Earning money by playing the sport you love is fantastic, and of course the rewards for doing so at the top are huge these days. But it's also true to say that the youngsters who are striving to make it and who have been taken on by professional clubs do not have it easy. Yes, they get to kick a ball around on a daily basis, they are given coaching and educational support by clubs and they have their feet on the bottom rung of that ladder they hope will lead to them being successful first-team regulars.

But there is also another side to their lives. They know from the moment they become an academy player that they have to continually prove themselves. They can't afford to stagnate or go backwards, and they have to be seen to be moving forward and developing into the finished article. Statistically they all know the chances of succeeding are slim, that the casualty rate in terms of kids not making it is very high, but each boy will enter that youth system believing that they are the one who will make it. They have to be able to maintain that belief and self-confidence day in, day out, because otherwise they know they will not stand a chance.

To have just reached that point the boys will have been scouted and looked at on a number of occasions by the club that takes them on. They will have been viewed as young footballers who have potential, but no more than that. Unless a kid is a Rooney or a Messi, no scout, coach or manager will be able to say with any degree of certainty that the player will make it. The competition has always been great, but it is perhaps even greater now.

In my day as a young player the majority of kids being signed by clubs were local. In fact the most exotic place one of West Ham's youngsters came from when I was a youth player was Liverpool! That was Alvin Martin. We also had two kids from Norfolk and one from Scunthorpe. All the rest, including myself, were local lads. I lived two miles away from West Ham's ground, but now top Premier

League and Championship clubs have worldwide scouting networks. There is a mixture of nationalities and cultures in an Under-18 dressing room just as there is in the first-team changing room. The best kids are not just scouted and looked at when they play in local school and parks teams as they were in my day – they can just as easily come from any part of the world, and the attraction of playing in England means that our clubs now have a much wider choice when it comes to making a decision about who they are going to take on. Their nets are cast much wider, and as a consequence I think the competition to make it as a professional is getting greater and greater. Although English clubs now scour the world, the same criteria apply: clubs will only look at top-quality youngsters with the skills, personality and ability that might one day make them into a first-team player.

FULHAM MIGHT NOT be Manchester United, Arsenal or Chelsea, but they are a club who spent thirteen consecutive seasons in the Premier League before being relegated in 2013. During that time they became an established top-flight team and were able to build the infrastructure that went with it. Their training ground and facilities are of a high standard, and their academy system is something they have worked hard at. Even though they have slipped out of the Premier League, they are still able to operate at a high level, and despite being not as large as some of the top teams their setup when it comes to recruiting and developing youth players is very good. Their academy was awarded Category One status in 2012 and their Under-18s have enjoyed success in recent years, winning their league. The academy itself is based at the club's training ground, giving the youngsters the chance to be in and around the same place where the first team train. This helps to promote the feeling that although the kids might just be starting out in their quest to earn their living as professionals, they are an important part of the club and its future.

If you were a youngster from West London or anywhere else in England, the prospect of getting the chance to join a club like Fulham would be both exciting and daunting. It would mean a lot of sacrifices and hard work, as well as possibly having to uproot from another part of the country to live in digs. It would be tough for any sixteen-year-old, so just imagine what it was like for Jón Thorsteinsson. He got the opportunity to realise his dream of being signed by the club, but at the same time he knew it would mean a complete change to his life. That's because Jón, as well as coping with all the other pressures that go with being a youngster trying to make the grade, had to say goodbye not only to his family but to his country as well.

Jón is from Iceland, and when he came over to England to join Fulham he did so knowing that he would have to leave his family and friends behind to pursue his dream of becoming a professional footballer in a foreign country. It doesn't matter how lucky you might think he was to have the opportunity – there's no denying that he had to make a brave decision and sacrificed an awful lot.

"When they first offered me a contract I didn't really think about having to leave home, but when it came to signing I wasn't sure," he admits. "I didn't want to sign. My parents said it was my choice and that they would be happy with whatever I wanted to do."

Jón was born in Reykjavík and has an older and a younger sister. He initially travelled to England to have trials, and Fulham obviously liked what they saw in his game and made an offer to sign him. He was already playing for a team in Iceland called HK Kópavogs so Fulham negotiated his release, enabling him to sign. When Jón reconsidered his decision, Fulham's academy director, Hew Jennings, completely understood the situation.

'Jón had some second thoughts,' says Hew, 'so we said, "Okay, stay a couple of weeks, take your time and you decide exactly what you want to do."' In the end Jón decided he wanted to stay and sign with the club. It was clearly difficult for him, but the thing that overrode everything was his desire to become a footballer in this country.

'The first week I was here after signing was a bit scary,' he admits. 'I had to get used to a lot of different things, including staying with another family and the routine of training with the club and playing games. One of the hardest things I've found is coming back to England when I've been home to Iceland for a visit. The first few days after I come back here are tough, because I've left my family and friends behind in Iceland, but the feeling doesn't last too long and then I get into life back at Fulham and everything is okay.

It's also easy to keep in contact with my family, not just on the phone but with things like FaceTime.'

Things have certainly moved on for young players both on the pitch and off of it. Although Jón may be a long way from home, having that ability to pick up his mobile phone or iPad to be able to see his parents and friends in Iceland must make things better for a young man living away from home for the first time. Like Jón, Alvin Martin had to live in digs when he first arrived at West Ham in the mid-1970s, but when he wanted to make a call home to Liverpool it meant a walk to the nearest phone box, because the family he was staying with didn't actually have a phone!

Fulham try to match the youngsters to families they think will be suitable for them. So if a kid is used to not having other children around the place at home they will look to house them with a similar family setup. After first being driven to the training ground, Jón and any of the other boys who are in digs are then encouraged to get to know the area better and use public transport to travel to and from training. His daily regime is a mixture of football, fitness and education, with the aim of gaining a BTEC and NVQ qualification, and this structure was something Jón adapted to very well. All the education is done in-house, and Jón's days not only include his football training, gym sessions and the education programme, but also English lessons to help bring his language up to speed. It's an awful lot to take on board for any youngster yet he seems to have coped with it well.

In addition to all the football and schooling, he also gets free time. 'It's good to have some time to go out with some of the other boys,' he says. 'There are also some Icelandic players that I am friends with who play for Reading, so whenever I can I will go over to see them, or they come over and we meet up.'

Just like the first-team footballers, the youth players have to adhere to certain diets, so the families who they lodge with are given special sessions by the club on just what sort of food the players should be eating. That doesn't stop Jón and his mates having the occasional treat at Nando's, but it's still a far cry from the way things used to be twenty, fifteen or even ten years ago. The whole setup at Fulham and at other academies is very professional. They give the boys they take in every chance to succeed in what is a very tough and competitive industry, but ultimately it's down to the individuals and the way they handle the constant need to progress and improve.

'When I first came and played in a game against Tottenham I found it very difficult,' admits Jón. 'It was a big shock. The tempo of the game was higher than back in Iceland, but I knew that I just had to get used to it and after a few weeks it settled down. I trained and got to know the different routines, and then I was able to cope better with the football and the games.'

Jón made good progress and at the age of sixteen found himself integrated into the Under-21 team on occasion, including a winning performance for Fulham in an away midweek match against West Ham at Upton Park. Games like these will stand out in any young player's mind for the rest of his life, no matter what he might go on to achieve, because when you play in them the matches are so exciting and vivid. It's really your first taste of the big time, playing in the sort of stadium you hope will become a regular part of your life.

'It was good to play at Upton Park and get the chance to play with the Under-21s,' he recalls. 'I played against some players who have played for the West Ham first team, including Joey O'Brien, who was marking me – and we won 2–0. It was a really good feeling, and after the game I called my parents in Iceland and told them all about the match and what had happened. It's good to get the chance to step up to a higher level, and it means I know more about what I have to do in order to make it. I think I've settled more into things and understand about having to keep working at my game and my fitness. I knew I had to get physically stronger to cope with what I had to do when I first came to England. To begin with that was tough, but it's got better and I think I've got stronger. You get used to things, and then they don't seem so strange or different. It's all part of what I have to do if I am going to become a footballer. I know lots of people want to be footballers, and that's been the case with me since I was very young. I had heroes like Eidur Gudjohnsen, and there have been other footballers from Iceland like Hermann Hreidarsson and Gylfi Sigurdsson who have done really well in the Premier League. I want to make it, but I don't feel any pressure from anyone else, like my family or friends. They want me to do well, but the only pressure I have is what I put on myself.'

Jón seems like an incredibly level-headed young man. His dedication and commitment to trying to become a footballer are fantastic. What he did in leaving home and basing himself in England at such a young age was a very big thing. He's already had to sacrifice a lot, but his determination to make it should be applauded. Of course he has ability, and his skill as a left-sided attacking midfielder clearly gave him the chance to join the Fulham academy, but being selected for the club was only the first step. I think he was very much aware that as soon as he signed for the club the real hard work began.

Football is a great business but it can also be a harsh business. I have seen so many really talented kids fail to make it as full-time professionals for one reason or another, and I know it can be heartbreaking for a player. As a manager it was never nice telling a youngster he was going to be released. I knew that for so many years the player had all his hopes and dreams focused on making it, and to be told that a club no longer wants you is a shock to the system. Some youngsters never recover from it and are lost to the professional game for ever; others may be late developers who might drop into non-league football and come back better and stronger for the experience.

I don't know what will happen to Jón in the future, but what I do know is that right now he is doing everything right – and by doing that he is giving himself every opportunity of achieving his aim of joining the likes of Gudjohnsen, Sigurdsson and Hreidarsson. The fact that Iceland, with a population of a little more than 300,000, has been able to produce some top-class players over a number of years is a story in itself. Who knows, perhaps in the next few years the name of Jón Dagur Thorsteinsson will be added to the list, and all the hard work and sacrifice will have paid off.

CHAPTER 6

ASSISTANT MANAGER/COACH

Ray Lewington

RAY LEWINGTON HAS pretty much done it all in football. He played the game professionally, he's been a manager, assistant manager and coach, and he's worked in an academy bringing youngsters through. But he's perhaps now best known to football fans as Roy Hodgson's assistant, a role he has fulfilled at both club level and as part of the England set-up.

Ray's qualities as a coach are well known in the game, and it was no surprise that Roy wanted Ray – together with Gary Neville – alongside him as assistant coach when he took over as the England boss in 2012. It's important for anyone in charge of a football team, whether it be at club or international level, to be able to rely on and have faith in the people who are assisting him. Having spent more than two seasons with Ray when Roy was manager of Fulham, Roy knew exactly what to expect, the two men having worked well as a team when they were in charge of the west London club. Ray helped Roy to rescue the team from what looked like certain relegation, and the side went from strength to strength in the seasons that followed, including a 7th-place finish and a European campaign that saw them reach the final of the Europa League in 2010 before losing 2–1 to Atlético Madrid after extra-time.

Having a good relationship between manager and assistant is extremely important to any football team, and certainly at club level the assistant manager is a role that is often undervalued and underestimated by many people. But having been a manager I know just how crucial it can be to have the right man around. I've always felt that the assistant manager takes a big weight off the manager, their job being to assist the manager in every way. That doesn't mean agreeing with him on everything – they should be there to offer an opinion on things – but once the manager makes his decision, the assistant has to go along with it and help him to carry it out. He's not there to contradict the manager, he's there to work alongside him, and to offer advice and support when needed. They are a team and as such have to show a united front.

'I think that one of the golden rules of the job is that whatever you say to each other or discuss behind closed doors in the office, once you go out and start dealing with the players you're singing off the same hymn sheet,' says Ray. 'There are some people who can't be a number two because they can't take other people's opinions. You've got to be able to say, "I might not agree with you, but if that's the way we're going to do things then let's go out and do them." It's the manager who has to make the decisions, and you have to go along with him and back him to the hilt.

'A manager has to be able to trust his assistant. If you're a manager and know things are going to be leaked and you're being undermined in what you're trying to do, it gets to the players. If the assistant or the coach just wants to be a friend to the players all the time and make little comments to them, you've got no chance. Roy knows I wouldn't do that, and because I've been a manager I know how important it is to have that sort of trust. I think that over the years the most successful number ones and number twos are the ones who have stuck together. They have become a team. I think a manager and his assistant have to have similar philosophies. There might be slight differences, but if one wants to play one way and the other wants to play a different way it just doesn't work.

'As a number two you have responsibility, but it's not the same as being a manager. As a manager, when you close that door to your office you're on your own. It doesn't matter if your assistant or the other people are backing you. At the end of the day you're on your own. I think it can be brutal being a manager and it can change you as a person. I don't think any other job in football does that. If you like coaching, then I think being assistant to a head coach is probably as good as you're going to get, but I also found that assistant manager suited me as well because I could be among players and sort things out, but I didn't have the ultimate responsibility.

'I don't think people realise the pressure that managers are under. As a manager you've got to answer to supporters, the board, the press, the players – there are so many roads that lead to you. Your head's full all the time and you end up thinking about everything apart from football! I think that's kind of what you lose as a manager, whereas when you're a coach you don't do that. As a coach I'll take on board problems, but I won't go home and have sleepless nights. I found that when I was a manager I couldn't sleep. As a coach that doesn't happen. As a manager I used to stay awake all night and I'd be writing things down. I'd be sitting downstairs in my house at four in the morning watching videos of matches. I don't do that as a coach or assistant manager. I'm still as passionate, and I think about everything that I'm doing with the team and the players, but I don't really lose sleep over it. The manager will, because the ultimate responsibility is his.

'The manager has to know that you're backing him, because when you get a case where your team has just lost three games on the spin you know that pretty much everyone else is against you. To do the job of assistant manager properly I think you have to do exactly what it says – you have to assist the manager, to help him. I think your remit allows you to do certain managerial things. For example, as an assistant if I felt the situation called for it I would have a word with a player. Maybe tell him to do himself a favour and start doing certain things to help him, whether it was the way he played or the way he acted. You do managerial things and not just football things. You can perhaps head off problems and you can take on board some of the managerial things with the permission of the manager, but the manager has to trust you.'

Although Ray has taken on all sorts of roles throughout his career, it's probably true to say that his first love is coaching, and it was something he began to think about when he was a player with Chelsea in the 1970s.

'I think coaching is probably the role that suits my personality best, because that's what I like doing most,' he says. 'I always wanted to coach. I wasn't a top player – I reached what would now be Championship level and was okay for what I was – but I always knew that I wanted to be a coach and I worked for it. I used to take the Chelsea kids for training on Tuesdays and Thursdays, and I also had good mentors. Dario Gradi was reserve-team manager at Chelsea and always kept prompting me to get my coaching badges, which I did. And then I had Ray Harford when I went to Fulham, and he did exactly the same. He was great. He was my favourite as a coach.

'I always thought I'd be a better coach than I was a player, so it was always my aim to become one. There's that thing on a Saturday when you get the end product, when the system is working well. So that if we lose the ball things work automatically, and people know exactly what they should do and where they should be on the pitch.

'I actually think that perhaps the best time I've had coaching was when I was involved in academies, because you can see players improve. Just by doing the little things, by putting little rules in place and seeing them do things they weren't doing before. That's when you think, "Yeah, I've made a contribution there." That sort of thing feels pretty good, and I would think academy coaches as a whole get a lot of satisfaction from what they're doing and seeing young lads improve.

'When a player gets in the first team, if he has a good coach he's really only going to improve by maybe 5 per cent. As a coach you'll do your main session, then you'll do your one-on-ones. Maybe you'll take two or three of the players and work with them just to give them more understanding and work on their technique, but there's not going to be rapid improvement. Things will improve, but it will be slowly, because by that stage the players know the bulk of what is needed. But it's different with kids. If you get a nine-year-old and at eleven they're doing things they weren't doing two years before, you can actually get some satisfaction and think, "I've been part of that, I've made him a better player."

'The best two coaches I ever worked under as a player were Dario and Ray. I could ask them anything, and they would make a point of doing something with me the next day that would help me. They made sense of everything for me. It wasn't just a case of them giving me instructions and leaving it at that. They would show me how you did things and they had enthusiasm for what they were doing all the time. They wanted to talk football and their quality of coaching was really good. They would also listen to you and physically go through things with you on the pitch. I never felt embarrassed about going to them and asking them to explain something to me. They were open and would be willing to explain things. They wouldn't put you down the way some coaches do. They would just get on and put on little sessions for you that would help your play.

'When I was in my mid-twenties at Fulham with Ray Harford, he would get five or six youth-team players together and get them to help me with different aspects of my game. Simple things like getting the ball and then getting it out of my feet quickly. So they would show you how to do things and they would listen to you. When I became a coach and a player-manager, Ray said to me, "Make training one for yourself and one for the players." So in other words, you did your work and then you maybe gave the players an eight-a-side game. It's a bit of light relief for them.'

In my experience I think there are two types of coaches, really. One is someone who has to get match-specific points across from Monday to Friday, perhaps doing something like showing a team how they are playing too deep and how they've got to go about getting higher up the pitch. This type of coach will put on sessions that replicate situations that the team find themselves in on a Saturday – and the players will then be able to see for themselves why they are doing the sessions. The other sort of coach is one that can put on entertaining sessions, because you can't have a situation where all the sessions are just work, work, work – you've got to mix the sessions up. So some sessions are just enjoyable and everyone gets something out of it, with the players having smiles on their faces. When you're doing match-specific sessions, there's no smiling going on because it's serious stuff. I think above all, the coach has got to get across what he wants during a session, and as you're walking off the training pitch you want the players to have grasped what you've just done and know why you've done it.

Ray has worked right across the football spectrum when it comes to coaching. He's coached kids, players from the lower end of the English leagues, players from the Championship and players from the Premier League. When Roy Hodgson asked him to be his assistant when he took the England job, Ray found himself thrust into a completely different way of working, with the chance to coach the cream of English footballers. As a coach at a football club you have that day-to-day rapport with the players, and you're there to try to improve them as individuals and build that bond that a coach has to have with his players. When you're taking a training session with a club side and that team has just been beaten for the third time on the spin, it's the coach who has to pick the players up and make sure the sessions have a bit of life about them. You have to lift the team and lift the individuals in that team. When it came to coaching the England players Ray was faced with a group who were already enthused, because they were in the England squad and were trying to get into the team to represent their country.

'It is very different to being a coach at a club,' he agrees. 'When Roy first asked me to join him after he'd got the job, he warned me that it would be very different for me because he knew how much I enjoyed having that day-to-day contact with players. So you do have to readjust the way you go about your life, and the time we actually have with the players and what we can do with them is very different. On a typical international week we might have them for eight days, but two of those days are matches, one is often at home and the other away, so there's all the travelling involved as well. When you break it down you don't really have the players on the training pitch for very long at all during that period.

'Roy is first and foremost a coach. He does all of his own coaching. I might do everything that comes off of that session, like the lead-in or the bit at the end, but it's Roy who will coach. In all the time I've worked for him I've only ever done two full sessions for him – one for England and the other for Fulham. Working for him is probably completely different to working for anyone one else, but he's a good man to work for because you can sit down with him and talk football. He's very open, and he wants to know your ideas and what you think.

'I suppose as an assistant I'm probably closer to the players than Roy is because there has to be that gap. With England you really don't get the chance to be a real number two in the sense that you would if you were with a club side. The fact that we only have them for that eight-day period means that it can be quite intense and manic, and when it finishes you're exhausted. I love coaching, and I think if I was twenty years younger I would have had to seriously think about doing the England job because of that lack of coaching involvement for long periods of time while you're in the job. It was a big change for me, but it's a great honour and I love coaching the England players. Time is everything with the international team, and you just don't get enough of it. Even things like going to see the opposition or potential opposition is difficult because we're pretty much playing on the same days as them.

'The other thing to remember is that we get a group of players who are all used to playing various systems and roles for their club sides, and we have to very quickly get them back doing what we want them to do for England. So you might get someone like Alex Oxlade-Chamberlain, who tends to play wide and stay wide when he plays for Arsenal, but when it comes to playing for England we wanted him to come in from the sides, getting in the pockets, and when we lost the ball there were different jobs to the ones he had at Arsenal. The players come, we have them for that period of time, we play two matches and then they go. We might not see them again for three, four or five months. The difference comes when you're involved in tournaments. Then it reverts to being much more like being involved with players at club level, because you're together day to day and you're playing matches every four days, something the players are used to doing with their clubs during the season.'

It's interesting, because people would consider that Ray reached the pinnacle of the coaching tree when he went to work with England – and in many ways that's exactly what he did. But you get the feeling that although it must be fantastic to work with the country's elite players, his career and the job he has done have never been about what type of player he has worked with. Ray just loves coaching, pure and simple, and perhaps that's best summed up by what he would like to do next.

'I'd like to go into the academies when I finish with England,' he says with certainty. 'Coaching comes into all sorts of categories, but my real satisfaction from being a coach is getting my points over and making it interesting at the same time. That sums it up for me, and that's what I hope I've always done as a coach.'

CHAPTER 7

AGENT

Jonathan Barnett

WHEN I WAS a player there was no such thing as an agent. You didn't really have anyone representing you when it came to transfers or contract negotiations. At West Ham I can remember being called in by the manager, Ron Greenwood, and being told, 'This is what you're getting.' I was in and out in less than five minutes, and there was no room for negotiation or debate. Some years later when I went to Aston Villa, who were the European champions at the time, it took about an hour for the whole deal to go through and the contract itself was about a page long. These days agents are always at the centre of any big transfer, negotiations can go on for months, transfer fees and salaries are into the millions, and a contract can consist of several hundred pages. Times have certainly changed.

The agent has now become an integral part of the football fabric of this country – and indeed of any other country that plays the game. It is a multi-million-pound industry and, like it or not, clubs, managers, chief executives and chairmen all have to deal with agents these days. I think it would be fair to say the public's perception of agents is not always favourable. They see them making a lot of money out of transfer deals and often wonder what exactly they do for it.

Gareth Bale is the most expensive player on the planet. His transfer in 2013 from Tottenham to Real Madrid cost the Spanish side a reported €100 million. The rumours that he would be leaving England for Spain began to circulate a year before the move actually took place, and when they gathered pace during the summer of 2013 the football world knew it was only a matter of time before he left White Hart Lane for the Santiago Bernabéu. It was just a matter of time – and negotiation. At the heart of these negotiations was Bale's agent Jonathan Barnett. The move to Real represented another phase in Bale's career, a client Barnett and his Stellar Group had looked after since the Welsh international was a youngster.

'We planned most things in Gareth's life,' says Jonathan. 'You can't plan that he's going to play for Real Madrid one day, but if the opportunity comes you do plan what you think is right for him at the time. When he went to Tottenham from Southampton, their offer wasn't the best one for him. It would have been more financially rewarding for him to go somewhere else. But we thought he should go to Spurs for various reasons. We look after our players – that's our role – and we look after them 100 per cent with everything except their on-the-field activities, because I don't think we should get involved in that.

'If you are a respected agent and you work properly, you can work with both sides. You don't earn money from both sides, but you can help the whole deal come together. I was with Daniel Levy, the Tottenham chairman, in many meetings, so I was privy to a lot of what was going on. There weren't secrets. We look after Gareth and negotiated on his behalf with Real Madrid. We came with a team of people, they came with a team of people and it gets worked out. When I started in the business a player's contract was literally a one-page appendix. Today it's 400 pages. Gareth is the most expensive player in the world and probably one of the best three players on Earth at the moment. He's an industry. It's all so different these days.

'Once the deal was done and the transfer went through, we took care of everything with Real Madrid to help with the move for Gareth. I think once you've dealt with Real Madrid you realise how big they are as a club – and how important they are. They dwarf any other club in the world. So it was even more difficult for him to get acclimatised. We had people there with him. We helped him to find a home, we negotiated the price of his home, we got all of his staff, we got his teachers to help him speak Spanish and we made sure there was somebody there at all times with him. He was never left alone. We got everything that was necessary to help him settle, and every few weeks my son Joshua would fly over and stay with him, so there was always someone there for us. We still run his household and we still do everything necessary for him.

'To be able to say I've done the biggest deal in history is fantastic, and people do look at me in a different light. I talked to a player abroad, and the mum and dad wanted to have their photograph taken with me. I'm not saying it was because they liked me, it was because they were thinking, "This is the guy who did the world record." I get a lot of that. Most of the young players abroad have their family take a picture with me.'

I've known Jonathan for quite some time, and probably one of my earliest recollections of him was when I was manager of Charlton Athletic and we sold midfielder Lee Bowyer to Leeds in a £2.8 million deal, which, at the age of nineteen, made him Britain's costliest teenager. Jonathan was Lee's agent at the time, and he admits that the business of being a football agent has changed enormously during that time. The days of an agent acting independently and having just a few clients are becoming numbered. These days the top agencies are big companies with big client lists. Jonathan and his partner David Manasseh run the Stellar Group, which in 2015 was listed tenth in the world's most valuable sports agencies, with estimated commissions of $44 million. It's a huge operation and they represent players from all over the world, a far cry from when he first started more than twenty years ago.

'I think we saw a need for agents,' he recalls. 'I think footballers were being used by clubs. I don't think they had good contracts. I'm proud that none of the players we represent will need to get a job when they finish with football. They can if they want to, obviously, but not because they have to. There's a misconception about this business, but there's agents and then there's agents. What people have to understand is that there are certain agents who call themselves agents, but what they do is trade. So they'll phone a manager up and say, "What are you looking for, who are you selling in January, who are you buying?" We don't do that. We, as a company, wouldn't even *try* that. We look after the players. We completely look after the player. We don't look after his finances because that's not correct, but we'll sit them down with top accountants and banks. We do everything else that's necessary so that they can concentrate on their football, but if they come to me and say they're unhappy because the manager criticised them I'll tell them to talk to him. I won't phone up managers. I could never say I was an expert on football – I'm a football fan and my job is to look after the players we represent.

'I remember once that one of our players was getting transferred, and the guy from our organisation who was looking after him was having trouble getting the deal done, so he asked me if I could speak to the chairman of the buying club. So I sat down with this particular chairman and told him what we wanted. He said, "Blimey, how good is he, John?" I said, "To be honest with you, I don't know if he's a striker or a goalkeeper. I haven't got a clue and why should I? You want him, your coach wants him and your scouts have seen him. All I'm saying is this is what my player wants to come here!"

'Our role is to look after the player. It's not for me to say to a chairman, "You've got to pay him because he's better than this this person or that person." My job is to look after the player – my client.

'We look after all of our players, and if we get players coming here from abroad we look after things like their houses and families. We have people in the company who speak six or seven languages and we've always got people who will spend time with the players. There are all sorts of things we do. Because of the money involved in the game these days, players can afford chefs. They can afford to be looked after properly. So we will find the chefs and they get food made properly so that when players come home they eat correctly. We liaise with the clubs, who will give dietary instructions to the chef. It's a massive job in terms of what we do for them, but it's important and that's why players come to us and we spend millions of pounds on scouting. If you gave me the name of one of our players, probably from the age of fourteen upwards, I could tell you what he had for lunch yesterday! But a lot of players will come to us because of who we are today.

'I can't deny it. I never dreamed in my life that David and I would be as successful as we are – and I thank God for it. But there are a lot of footballers who have made a lot of money through us. We're not ashamed of our success. We don't flaunt it, we're very happy with what we've got. I think as long as players think we've done a good job for them then that's great.'

It's all a far cry from Jonathan's early days as an agent, when one of the people originally involved in the business was Les Sealey, someone I knew quite well and who I played alongside in a Sunday-morning team when we were kids growing up. Les was a real character and played in goal for Manchester United, Coventry and West Ham, among others, before tragically dying from a heart attack in 2001 at the age of forty-three.

'I came from a business background and knew nothing about football, but I knew Les – and he was fantastic for us,' says Jonathan. 'The deals today are so much more complicated. There are so many things that can go into a contract and so many things that you might want taken out of them. I'm coming at it differently from clubs. I want flexibility, so that if things don't work out the player can get out or if he outgrows the club he can go somewhere else. I want to know he's going to be looked after, that he's not going to walk into the changing room and be the lowest-paid player there. It's more important for me that he's not the lowest-paid player than it is that he's the highest-paid. You have to make sure you get it right – and it's so technical with things such as image rights, then there are major corporations who have deals with players, and you even get things like how many times a year the player will mention a particular product.

'There are guys in the world today who are earning £20 million or £30 million a year – you're talking about massive amounts of money – so you have to know what you're doing. I love to negotiate deals. Did I enjoy it more years ago? Yes, I had more contact with people like managers. Now it's much more chief executives.'

As in any business, Jonathan believes there are good and bad operators when it comes to agents, but that a lot of the bad ones could be excluded from operating if there were tighter rules and regulations in place. He also believes the role of the agent is bigger and more complex than it has ever been when it comes to dealing with players and clubs.

'You should have proper training to be an agent,' he insists. 'I want rules to be stronger and I want to make them better. I want them to be relevant to what we do. You get people calling themselves "intermediaries" and operating in the business. The problem is that the FA and FIFA actually don't know what an agent does. Nobody from the FA has ever set foot in my office and asked me what an agent does, or what goes on.

'Young players should look to go to an agent who will help them. We manage their expectations. You can't sit down with a player and say you've just spoken to Manchester United, and then tell him that they want him and in two years he'll definitely be going to play for them unless you know that's a fact. You'd be mad. But that's when you get bad agents who might promise something that's unrealistic and that's when you get kids fed up with life. You've got to tell them the truth.

'I also think the most successful clubs in the world are the ones that work properly with agents. They don't fear them – they work with them. The ones that are less successful are the ones that think they know better than the agents. You hear them shout, "There's too much money being spent on an agent." Well, I don't remember Real Madrid ever saying that, or Barcelona, or Bayern Munich. They don't shout that they pay too much. They pay good money and they get great results. I think if you work with clubs it comes out okay.'

Jonathan and the Stellar Group may be best known for the Bale transfer, but as well as a player like him and other well-established footballers they also look after a lot of young players who are trying to make their way in the game. It can be difficult for a lot of youngsters to make that vital breakthrough, particularly at some of the bigger Premier League clubs, and sometimes they might have to try their luck out on loan. Making the right decision can be crucial.

'I actually think that a kid who doesn't want to come to this company has got to be raving mad,' says Jonathan. 'As long as they listen to me and what I say, I'll look after them. But if they don't listen and want to do their own thing, then we're not there for them. Over the years we've come across most things and several times we've been in court on a Saturday taking out injunctions. We've got a fleet of lawyers and we're very well organised. But we're also more selective. If we think a player is going to be bad for our company then we'll turn them away and tell them to sign for another agent. I don't have a problem with that. If they sign with us they sign for two years and then re-sign if they want to. If anybody wants to leave us and it's for a legitimate reason, I'll let them go.

'To send a young player to the Championship is a waste of time because they're not going to play young players in the Championship. The rewards are so big – they want experienced players. The primary question is whether the player will get the chance to start or play every week. I think the answer is no, but if the player says that he wants to go and play there I'll never overrule him. It's his decision at the end of the day. Maybe he'll listen to me, maybe he won't. I'd say that 99 per cent of the time it's not a conflict with the clubs. The big clubs are pretty right with what they want to do. Very rarely will we have an argument. They've got very good schemes to move out their young players.'

Football has never been bigger and, as a business, it has never been richer. The Stellar Group and Jonathan Barnett are big players in a very big game. In 1961 eyebrows were raised when Fulham's Johnny Haynes became the first £100-a-week footballer after the abolition of the £20-a-week maximum wage. Can Jonathan see the day when a footballer will be paid £1 million a week?

'I don't think the bubble's going to burst. Football's getting bigger and bigger, and salaries will get bigger and bigger,' he says. 'So yes, someone getting paid £50 million a year? I think that will come very shortly.'

One thing's for sure. If that day does come, you can bet that right at the heart of such a deal will be the player's agent.

CHAPTER 8

CHIEF EXECUTIVE

Phil Alexander

PHIL ALEXANDER IS one of the longest-serving chief executives in English league football. He has been with Crystal Palace for twenty years, during which he has worked with sixteen managers and four different club owners, and has twice experienced the difficulties associated with going into administration. It's probably fair to say that when it comes to being the chief executive at a football club, Phil has seen it, done it and bought the T-shirt. As chief executive of the club he has been one of the few constants behind the scenes at Palace and has had to deal with all sorts of things during his time there. He has experienced the euphoria of promotion to the Premier League via the nail-biting play-off route, as well as the sadness of being beaten in one of those finals. He has had to deal with relegation from the top flight and has had to sit through the drama of avoiding the drop on the last day of the season.

Right through it all he has had to use his expertise to try to do what is best for the club in what have often been difficult times. For the past three seasons Palace have established themselves in the Premier League, and the days when they were labelled a 'yo-yo' club now seem to be behind them. There seems to be a stability about the club that perhaps wasn't there in the past, and as a result they are flourishing and a new chapter is opening up for Phil in his long association with them. But because of his past experiences he is perhaps more aware than most of the need to be prudent and build the club with sturdy underpinnings.

'The club looks more stable – and it is more stable – but football's football and you've always got to be aware of the potential for the worst-case scenario,' he insists. 'We're in a position now where the club has some solid foundations. We're planning – but we need to get the finances in place, we need to have the infrastructure in place and we can't take risks. We need to have a plan for the stadium development that could withstand the financial impact of relegation. You can't stand still because if you stand still you will fall behind. You've got to have ambition and move forward. We have a slogan that we use at the club, "Ambition with Integrity", which means we want to do the best we can, we want to go on and play European football, but we'll do it in the right way and we'll not do it by cutting corners. So you can be ambitious – but you've got to do it in the right way. You cannot take risks and you've always got half an eye on what the downsides are and ask, "What could go wrong here if we do that?" You have to take care of those downsides, but at the same time still push on, if you do that you pretty much get it about right.'

When Phil joined Palace Ron Noades was the owner and chairman of the club. In the summer of 1998 he sold Palace to Mark Goldberg, but by the spring of the following year the club went into administration. In 2000 Simon Jordan became the new owner but ten years later Crystal Palace found themselves in administration once more, and in the end it was a consortium of four businessmen, Steve Parish, Martin Long, Stephen Browett and Jeremy Hosking, who rescued the club. The four also happened to be Palace fans, and in 2013 the club returned to the Premier League after eight years in the Championship. Since then they have gradually been building behind the scenes and on the pitch. At the end of last year it was announced that two wealthy Americans, Josh Harris and David Blitzer, would be investing in the club, with co-chairman Parish acting as the operating co-owner. So it appears there could now be exciting times ahead for Palace and, as chief executive, Phil Alexander can expect to be involved with pretty much everything that goes on at Selhurst Park.

'I suppose that as a chief executive you're ultimately responsible for the management of the business on behalf of the shareholders,' he explains. 'How tight the money is – and the resources you have available – will depend on what league you're in. I've been through times here where there have been very limited resources. The ultimate was when we were in the administration periods. When the administrator comes in his job is to run the business, keep it going as best he can in the short term and get the best he can for the creditors. So you've got to keep the business going to give it value, and that value goes back to the old creditors – but you can only spend what money you generate. You can get rid of costs, but any football debts, such as players' money and money owed to any other club, have to be paid 100p in the pound. During an administration period it really is hand-to-mouth and you quickly find out who your friends are.

'As a chief executive you have responsibility for all parts of the business, even in areas where perhaps you don't feel so skilled or comfortable. But as a result of that – of those tough times – I've obviously got a very broad knowledge of the business. Everything from running a match day through to the health and safety issues, running a stadium, running the stewarding operation through to the commercial side of bringing revenue in, which is probably my core strength. There are also transfer and contract negotiations with clubs, transfer and contract negotiations with agents and players, and knowing all the rules and regulations that go with all of that to ensure the club are fully compliant.

'I was also a professional footballer at Norwich City as a young man, so I kind of get the culture. I can talk the same language and I know what a dressing-room environment is like. I didn't appreciate it at the time but this actually does help when you're at the training ground, as it can be quite an intimidating place. So during administration I got a really broad knowledge of the business because we didn't have that many people and you just had to get on with it. I had to learn it all. Effectively, you've got half a dozen businesses within a football club that generate money. Things like the box office and ticketing operation, the retail operation, corporate sales and business hospitality, advertising, catering, managing the training ground. You had to take full responsibility.

'But as we mature and maintain our Premier League status you want to grow and bring in specialist expertise in those areas. We're now going through that growth and we've got some great people on board. There's no need for me to be quite so hands-on, but I need to be across every department. I retain certain elements of what I've always done, but then there are other things that take up my time. Certainly the club transfer negotiations and the player negotiations with agents are key. Last summer I spent a month of my life going backwards and forwards with PSG when we were buying Yohan Cabaye. They were tricky negotiations and quite complex. PSG knew what they were doing and so did we, so it just takes a lot more time, but I'm happy to do that. It's a bit of a game of poker at times, but we got him in the end and he's been a fantastic asset. Our manager Alan Pardew and the chairman Steve Parish decided they wanted to go for him – they then set the parameters of the deal. Then it's a case of me getting the deal done. Steve and Alan were informed of the progress throughout the process, and I had to make sure every detail was thought through and negotiated as best as possible in our favour.

'Lots of things have changed during my time as chief executive here but some things have stayed the same. For example, the most important relationship in any club is the manager and the chairman – absolutely no doubt about that, it has to be rock solid. One represents the boardroom and the shareholders, and the other represents the training ground and the players. It's absolutely key to the success of any club, but other things contribute to that as well. If you've got the chairman, manager, players, fans and local media facing the right way you can do some fantastic things, when everyone is going in the same direction. But when you get one of those factions suddenly changing direction, whether it's the fans, whether it's the players, the chairman or the manager, you lose a cog and you start to wobble a little bit. You're not going forward and suddenly you can find yourself going backward.'

I've often thought that a chief executive can also act as a bit of a buffer between the manager and the chairman. He has the ear of both, and also has to deal with the finances involved with the smooth running of the club. Phil is the person who has to talk to the manager about money and transfers. It can often be tricky because as a manager you might feel you need a particular player at a particular time, but the club also have to weigh up the fact that they must work within their means and cannot afford to overstretch themselves financially.

'We set the budgets and, yes, I've had the level of conversation in the past where if a manager wants to get someone in, we have to get someone out first. But generally the manager gets it,' he says. 'They'll push and they'll always want that one more player, and that's understandable. But at the end of the day the club's finances are finite, and you've got to make it work, otherwise you end up going onto rocky ground and into administration. The Premier League is a fantastic machine – the construction and structure of the league mean the distribution of revenues is equitable, and the revenues that we get from television are far greater than from other parts of our business. So the revenues of all the clubs have gone up because of TV, and it has a great levelling effect. If you do get relegated you get parachute payments that are designed to keep the business going and to get you back up at some point.

'I've got a real passion for the business, and some people might say that I'm a little too tight when it comes to doing deals. But I've got to be careful with the pennies. I know what it's like to live hand-to-mouth in a very difficult situation. We always build a relegation clause into players' contracts. I've had agents say to me, "No, we're not doing that," but you've got to be prudent. You've got to think that way, and we absolutely insist on it. The time you stop thinking about that and you don't put those fall-back positions in is the time you'll come a cropper. When it comes down to negotiations we're not going to risk the future of the club, and everyone buys into that; the manager, players, supporters, sponsors – everyone's on the same page.

'You've got to protect the soul of the club, and that's one of the things that the current owners do very well. You've got to protect the things that are important to the club and that's what Steve does. He knows what we're all about. We're not about sticking the prices up, fleecing everybody and making as much money as we can. We want to make match day a really exciting event, a real family day, and keep the ticket prices as competitive as possible. We want to make sure the place is accessible, make sure the owners are accessible, do what we can in the community and make sure we don't lose the heart of the club. If players get too far away from supporters or the owners are distant, people don't feel that they're getting listened to. Supporters don't feel that what they say is important and they do not feel as connected.'

As chief executive at Palace it's clear that Phil is involved in many different aspects of the business, but the role of the chief executive can vary depending on the club.

'I don't think you'll get any clubs with the same structure,' he insists, 'so you don't get any club where the role is exactly the same. Some chief executives don't get involved in the football side of the business at all – they just run the business side of the operation, which is absolutely fine. Then you might have a director of football doing all the deals and reporting to the chairman. I've been in football all my life in one shape or form, from non-league level right the way through to the Premier League, but other chief executives have skills that I probably don't have, such as working in a PLC.

'As a chief executive I've always tried to give the owner and the shareholders the benefit of my experience and expertise over the years, and perhaps give them a different view to how they see it. I feel to be true to myself I have to say that. If I just stood by and let it go I wouldn't be true to myself. They will generally ask my opinion and I'll give it, but if they choose to go against my views and do their own thing I'll support them all the way. Ultimately they pay the wages – it's their business and I'll support that.

'To be absolutely frank, Steve Parish has led from the front and he's taught me a lot of things. It's not a case of me being here a long time and therefore I know everything. I'm sure some of the things I've talked about to Steve and the other lads, they've thought, "Thanks very much, we'll do it." Equally, they've come up with things that I've not thought of myself. I've continued to learn on this particular journey. The combination is healthy for the business and all the individuals.

'When they came in 2010 it was the start of a new chapter for the club, with Steve taking the lead and the other three investors, all very wealthy individuals in their own right and really good people. It's worked, but it would be difficult to create that at another club. You couldn't take it as a model and go to another club and say, "Right, I've seen what those guys have done over there. Let's re-create that here." It's not a precise recipe.'

One of the other things that has to work for a club to progress and achieve success is getting the right manager. Having worked with so many during his time at the club, Phil is acutely aware of the importance of choosing the right man for the job. Managers come and go. More often than not they leave because the club sacks them, but they may also go because another club comes in for them or because they choose to resign. It's an important moment for any club – and particularly for one like Palace, who are trying to establish themselves as part of the Premier League fabric. I once had a conversation with a chief executive who told me that when he was signing a new manager he was actually thinking ahead as to who he might want to sign next, because he felt he always had to be prepared for what might happen. So I wondered what Phil's thoughts were on the matter.

'When it comes to choosing a manager, the example I use is to say it's a bit like a cocktail barman,' he says. 'The barman has got to make a drink that's made up of a lot of different components, but it has to taste right. In a way what you're trying to do is make that drink your club, and putting the manager in there with the other components means that he has to be right for that drink to taste the way you think it should. When you're looking for a manager you have to think about what you want from them. So you might think, "Where are we? We're bottom of the league, so we need fighting qualities. Or we're in the Premier League, so we need someone who's got Premier League experience and we need someone who has got good man-management skills to work with senior players."

'So the manager fits that particular drink at that particular time, but because he doesn't fit the drink and doesn't make the cocktail taste right it doesn't mean he's a bad manager. It just means that he's not the right ingredient for that cocktail at that particular time. It's very difficult to get all the ingredients right to make that drink – you have to consider the fans, the players and the chairman, and where the club are at that particular moment in time. Is he the right person for that drink? We've made choices right the way down the track and thankfully we've done pretty well, choosing the managers at the right time for the growth of the club.

'Appointing Alan in 2015 was a massive decision. Steve was adamant he was the right man for the job. With Alan's experience and his background with the club as a player, he was someone who could take the club forward and who could take it on. It's been absolutely the right choice.

'When you're negotiating a manager's contract it's probably only the first or second time you've met him, and you're with his lawyer or representative and you're planning the marriage of him and the club. But at the same time you've got to plan for the divorce! It's quite tricky, really, because you're talking about a manager leaving in a contractual context and he hasn't even got his foot in the door. So that isn't easy when you're starting a relationship. You've got to plan the marriage and the divorce at the same time in a contract, and you're trying to build a relationship with the new manager. That's just the way it is, and you have to do that. But in terms of me planning for the next manager? No, I've no reason to do that. No reason to plan it.'

What seems clear is that no two chief executives do the job in the same way. There's no right or wrong way to go about it, but there's also no doubt that the job has a hugely significant role to play in the modern game. To have been doing it for twenty years at the same club shows the importance of someone like Phil Alexander to Palace. He knows the job inside out and he knows the club. No doubt his experience and skills as a chief executive will continue to be an asset to them if they are to continue developing as a Premier League team.

CHAPTER 9

BACKROOM

Wayne Diesel, Nick Davies, Steve Rigby,
Mark Maunders

THERE ARE SO many things that go on behind the scenes at a football club to enable it to function properly. It would be impossible to highlight all of them, and it would be wrong to say that one job is more important than another, but there's no doubt that the head of medical and sports science has an increasingly significant role to play in many clubs these days. It's a role that is relatively recent, and one that we used and benefitted from some years ago when I was at Charlton. In 2003 when we appointed Wayne Diesel as head of medical it was something that was new for us as a club, but it was a role that Wayne had already performed for Gloucester rugby club. He was vastly experienced in a whole variety of sports apart from rugby and was able to bring a fresh approach not only to the way that we dealt with injuries, but also to injury prevention and the recovery time that players needed.

We were a Premier League club, but we were a small Premier League club and didn't have the money and resources of other bigger, more glamorous clubs. Upgrading our medical department in the way that we did certainly helped the club, and I think it also helped the players, who were introduced to some completely new methods of preparation and recovery. Wayne stayed at Charlton for four years before going on to become head of medical and sports science at Tottenham for eight years, working with six different managers during that time. In 2015 he opened a new chapter in his career when he took his skills across the Atlantic to become sports performance director with the Miami Dolphins in the NFL.

I vividly remember one of the big changes he made when he first arrived at Charlton. This was the introduction of ice baths, which were pretty much unheard of in the world of football at the time. The reason I remember it so well was because of Paolo Di Canio's reaction to being asked to jump into one after training. Paolo, who had come to us in the summer of 2003 from West Ham, was a big signing and a big star at the time. We didn't actually have any baths that we could fill with ice, so Wayne improvised using large refuse skips that we had at the training ground. The players were asked to get in them, and I knew that if Paolo jumped in the others would follow because of who he was. But he didn't just jump in as asked. Instead he asked Wayne why he should do so.

Wayne explained the whole thing to him and the thinking behind the idea, that it was all part of making sure players recovered better after exercise. I stood behind Wayne while he went through all the benefits of this new recovery programme, thinking that I really didn't want to have a row with the players on the first day of pre-season training. But once it had all been explained to him Paolo got in, and the other players soon followed his example.

'What was striking to me was the fact that it was so unusual,' recalls Wayne. 'I come from South Africa and had been involved in all sorts of sports with Olympic teams, and then when I was at Gloucester rugby it was a normal part of recovery. So what was surprising for me was that I had to explain it at all, because I'd been doing it for so long.'

The ice baths were just one of the new ideas and methods that Wayne brought with him, and he definitely had an influence at the club and the way in which the players were looked after, streamlining the medical and sports science departments.

'Because of my background with sports science we managed to bring the two departments together. One of my key jobs with a lot of organisations, even with the Dolphins now, is to try and bring together sports science and the medical, because often they don't talk and there can be two camps. At Tottenham we evolved the whole thing where I looked after doctors and sports scientists, everyone. So there was the club doctor, the head physio – and he'd look after the massage therapists – and we had pedicurists, chiropodists, osteopaths and chiropractors, and then we had sports science. So that would be your strength and conditioning coach as well as your analysts, who were looking at all the data we were getting from the players while they were training – the GPS data and the game data. So we had all of that going on and it was my job to make sure we had co-ordination between all of those departments. We said, "Right, let's make it one department so that the players hear one voice instead of several different ones."

One voice that some players will want to hear – and which can become a problem for a club – is that of a physio, doctor or some other specialist who is not part of the club, but who the player wants to go off and see.

'That can be a difficulty,' admits Wayne. 'It can happen, particularly with foreign players who might want to see someone in their own country or someone who has been recommended to them by their agent. They can end up going to different parts of the world. I know a colleague at another Premier League club who once told me, "Wayne, I'm acting as a travel agent. All I'm doing is arranging flights."

'I always wanted to be with the player if he was seeing someone, and at Tottenham we did it in a slightly different way because we brought the specialists to us. We would say, "You come and see the player, but let us see what you're doing." I'd then tell the therapist at the club what this guy was doing and what he wasn't doing. I would say to the physios and other people in the department, "You get on with looking after the fit players." It meant that I could take the injured players out of the loop, make sure they got a programme that was going to make sure they recovered properly and then put them back into the loop again.

'Players will sometimes tell the manager they're okay to play when they're not, and the manager's under so much pressure and is thinking that he has to win the next game. But I was employed by the club not the manager. I had to look after the club, I had to look after the manager, but most importantly I had to look after the player. The high turnover of managers makes it harder for the head of medical. It's important to have continuity, because the players want continuity and the club wants that continuity. Managers will sometimes want their own fitness coach to come with them when they get a job, but it's the department as a whole that needs to stay the same. When I was at Tottenham I had lots of conversations with Daniel Levy, the chairman, and he supported me through all the changes of manager we had. I know there were pressures on him because some of the managers who came in wanted their own thing, they wanted things to change. But Daniel said no, and that was great for us as a department.'

Tottenham are in the process of planning their move to a new stadium that will have a capacity of more than 60,000, and in recent years they moved into a training complex in Enfield with tremendous facilities that is the envy of many Premier League clubs. When he was at Spurs Wayne had a big part to play in the planning of the training complex, and he also had an input when it came to plans for the new stadium.

'I had a huge say in the planning for the training ground,' he says. 'I was very conscious of making sure we got things to flow from the moment the players went in for training each morning. So what we looked at was what the player does in his daily life when he's training. He'll obviously come in and go to the changing room, so I wanted to make sure there was a medical room that was adjacent to it that they could go into if they're doing recovery. Everything needs to flow, so there was a big input from the medical and sports science staff and from the manager as to what would be best, what would make the players feel comfortable in their environment.

'We also wanted to have a swimming pool because players will often use this as part of their recovery programme. It was going to be put at a level below the gym, but I didn't want it below ground and without light. We got them to excavate the ground underneath the gym, so that the pool could be built with natural light shining into it – and this cost as much as the pool itself! But it's now one of the star attractions. When I came over to London last September for a game that the Dolphins were playing at Wembley against the New York Jets I took some of the staff from the NFL there, and they said how wonderful the pool was.

'I was already working on the new ground before I left Tottenham, and once again it was about trying to get that flow and what could be in it from the medical and sports science point of view. If you go inside the stadium at Porto they've got a full-blown medical facility, and during the week the community can use it. They've got specialists there, they've got scanners and a gym – all sorts of facilities and equipment – and they can do things like a pre-signing medical there. They've got parking available, and they're utilising that stadium right through the week. Then on game days they obviously close it down and the public can't use it, but if the players get injured during a match they've effectively got a hospital in the stadium. I thought this was a genius idea. They've also got a university attached, so that was part of what I was talking to Tottenham about. It was one of the things that attracted me to the Dolphins, because their training facility is right in the middle of a university campus. So you've got interns and students coming in who can help out with testing and screening. And they can analyse data, too, because if you're in a busy medical department you don't have time to analyse all the data in the way they can.'

I found it interesting that the Dolphins should look to someone like Wayne to help improve the way they look after their players. Lots of people in this country would probably think that the Americans in the NFL are way ahead of us when it comes to their medical and sports science departments. But as Wayne explains, it seems this is not necessarily the case.

'The Americans typically think that their way is the best way, but coming over here in recent years and playing games at Wembley as part of their season – I think it's opened their eyes. I suppose I'm proof of that. I think it's why people like myself have been asked to go there with some of the ideas we have and the things we've learnt. They've been amazed at how advanced we are with some of the medical stuff and the sports science – how we're doing it. I think the brief when they recruited me was to get someone from outside the NFL to bring a fresh approach.

'Going back to something like the ice baths, they just don't have them after a game. These guys can be showered and changed in ten minutes, and gone. They don't have things like the individual drinks that Premier League players will have. Part of it is the sheer numbers in the locker room, so instead of getting an individually made-up drink that is tailored to that player's requirements as part of his recovery programme, they all just get a Gatorade. But now we've got a nutritionist and I'm working with her to tailor the drinks to the individuals in future, with the players' name and number on the bottle, just like we did at Tottenham.

'They may not have relegation, but it is brutal the way that coaches will lose their jobs if they're not successful and players get cut at the beginning of the season. At the start of a pre-season we will typically have over ninety players, but before the season starts forty of them will get cut. That's it – out the door. The other thing that is very different is how physically tough the training is in terms of weight loss. The Dolphins will typically train in temperatures of between 36 and 38°C, so they lose incredible amounts of fluid. They can lose between fourteen and sixteen pounds during a session, so they get drips. If they're dehydrated they get put on an IV with fluids. This is not allowed in England and the rest of the world, but it's accepted in the States – partly because you have to hydrate these kids.

'When it comes to injuries it's the joints that take a battering in the NFL – impact injuries, just like in rugby. In soccer they have 'over-use' injuries – the tendons, the wear and tear, grinding away. So you can get things like arthritic hips and ankles. They say that American football is tough, but soccer is harder. You can't repair a frayed tendon. You can't repair a joint that is ground down to sawdust. If you break a bone you can repair that, but degenerative conditions that footballers have here are tough.

'When I first went into soccer, rugby was way ahead in the way it looked at players and what could be done from a medical and sports science point of view. That has changed now – as the game has become more and more valuable, the players have become more valuable. I've never understood why we don't treat the body of an athlete the way we would treat an F1 engine, where you have to monitor and record every little aspect of it to get to the best possible performance out of it. Technology is moving forward all the time.

'In the future – and I don't think it's that far away – we'll be able to insert a little chip into a player and as they walk through the door in the morning there will be equipment that will pick up from that chip all the vital data we need. It'll check the heart, how well they've slept, their level of hydration – all sorts of things that will be useful in making sure the player is properly looked after and performs as best he can.'

It all makes those days of our ice baths at Charlton seem like a very long time ago.

* * *

NICK DAVIES WAS someone else who was with me at Charlton. A specialist in sports science, he joined us straight from university and worked alongside Wayne. He worked for me again when I was at West Ham, then he went on to Birmingham City, and since 2013 he has been head of sports science at Norwich City. It's a big job for anyone at a football club these days, and the attention to detail that is involved in making sure players are looked after physically and can perform at an extremely high level each week has greatly advanced from the days when he started – even if it was only thirteen years ago. I wanted to get a sense of what the job involved for him on a daily basis, and perhaps the best way to illustrate this is by looking at his working week, which begins just minutes after the team comes back into the dressing room after playing a match on a Saturday.

'I think the one thing that's moved on tremendously since I first started is the recovery side of what we do,' he says. 'The recovery programme for the next game needs to start literally the moment the final whistle goes. After the game the players are split into two groups: those who have played and those who haven't. The ones who haven't played might have the hump, but they still need to work out on the pitch. We also have bikes with us in the changing room so that the players can spin their legs out for ten minutes.

'Nutritionally, they've all got their specific drinks and bars, which are all bespoke to them, with different levels of carbohydrate and protein in them. We've gone away from having food in the changing room because it was a bit haphazard. So for home games the players will actually go up to the players' lounge and have their set food. For away games the coaches we travel in are so brilliantly kitted out that they can have their food while on the move, and the menu is worked out between me, the nutritionist and the chef who prepares the food. They're also all weighed in and out before the game and after it, and they have a fluid prescription depending on what they've lost during a game. If they've lost a kilogram in body weight, then they have to put one and a half litres of fluid back into their system. We've found the average weight loss is around two kilograms, so that means they need to take onboard three litres of some kind of electrolyte sports drink. After all of this they're given guidelines on how they should conduct themselves, what food they should have and what they're doing with their bodies.

'On the Sunday when they come into the training ground after a game they're again split into two groups: those who didn't play and those who did. The players who did will go through a batch of recovery processes – things like massage and electro-stimulation, where they'll have pads strapped to their legs and it helps to flush all the waste products out. On the Monday those who have played will typically get the day off, and that gives me and my staff the opportunity to go over all the data we've got from the game at the weekend. What we've found over the years is that someone who hits their personal best in a game or is close to it – they always seem to be the ones who are susceptible to picking something up. So we work a traffic-light system. If someone's gone past their personal best they get flagged as red, if they've got near to it then it's yellow, and below that it's green.'

All the data Nick has at his disposal will then form the basis of how he thinks a player might react physically during the coming week of training. Certainly in the past this could have caused a conflict with the manager, who might have wanted to work with a player who had played to his limit in the previous game. The manager might have wanted to do a high-intensity session, but the sports science people would say they didn't think he should be involved in that sort of training because of the risk of him picking up an injury. In years gone by not all managers would have wanted to take that sort of advice. It might be that he'd had a terrible result at the weekend and was determined to push his players in training – but that's when you can start to lose them with injuries. So I think that Tuesday morning after everything has settled down after the weekend is one of the most vital days of the week, because that's when a manager wants to get back to coaching his squad in preparation for the next game.

'I would say that there are now more managers who are willing to listen to the advice that a sports science department can give,' says Nick. 'Things have changed in recent years, but I do know that not every manager wants to listen – and when you talk to people at other clubs you do hear some horror stories. At Norwich, when they come in on a training day they'll arrive at 9.15 in the morning and go through a battery of tests to give us an indication of where they are physically. We call it "pre-training testing", and once a week we'll take a blood prick, which will give a marker of fatigue. We do a heart-rate sample for a minute, which can show fatigue in the system, we have a flexibility test, a hydration test and we check body weight. We also have a "wellness questionnaire", which is very simple. It has things on it like, "How many hours did you sleep and what was your sleep quality? Do you feel ready to train? Do you feel fatigued?"

'Sometimes a player might not feel right, and the answer to why that is the case can be very simple. For example their partner might have just had a baby, and that might mean their sleep has been interrupted and they're not properly rested because they've been up with the baby in the middle of the night. The big thing for me is to try to get the players on the training pitch all the time, not to keep pulling them off it. I think a good sports scientist highlights the issues with a player, rectifies them and stops the player having to be pulled out of the training session. When you start to do high-speed running and sprinting, and the legs are at top speed, that's when you're most susceptible to muscle injuries. So we do all the small stuff on a Tuesday and the bigger stuff on a Wednesday. Every training night – and the night before a game – they'll be given their nutritional pack. This will have an electrolyte drink in it and also a slow-releasing protein drink, so that while they're sleeping they release energy – they'll drink those just before they go to sleep.'

Nutrition – just what a player puts into his body – is a big part of the modern game, and it's all geared towards making sure players can perform at their best. The days of having a few pints in the players' bar after the game – and maybe eating fish and chips on the coach after an away game – are long gone. The chef has an important role to play in making sure that the food the players eat is cooked and prepared in the right way and with the right ingredients. When I was manager at West Ham the chef would prepare dinners for the young single boys, so that we knew they were getting to eat the right food each night. On one occasion he even prepared a Christmas meal for one player because his mum and dad were coming for lunch and his girlfriend couldn't cook it. He prepared everything for them, and all they did was heat it up!

'We've even had the partners of players come in and do a cooking lesson with our chef,' says Nick. 'That way they can see exactly how food should be prepared, even if it's something like grilling instead of frying. The majority of players who live on their own have also learned how to cook for themselves and prepare meals in the right way. Those who don't cook for themselves are given a made-up pack for their evening meal.

'When we get to the Friday the manager will do his "shape" with the team, but it's done at walking tempo. So although he's still able to get his points across as to what he wants them to be doing in the match the next day, it means that he's not taking anything away from the players physically twenty-four hours before they're going to play.

'On the morning of a match the players will all have to come down for breakfast, they have a urine test to make sure they're hydrated and then after breakfast they'll rest in their rooms, but within that there's a choice, just as there is when they have their post-match meal. The pre-match meal is at 11.45 for a 3pm kick-off, and that meal can be based on the urine sample we took earlier. We turn up at the ground at 1.30, the players will go out and have a look at the pitch, and then when they come back that's when their supplement programme begins – and they'll be taking different supplements that are tailored to them. At 2.20 they go out on the pitch to do their warm-up, which will include dynamic-flex exercises, sprints, footwork and some possession play. At 2.47 they need to be on their way down the tunnel and back to the changing room, and then just before they go out for the match we give them caffeine, which is a stimulant, and then they're away and onto the pitch for the match.'

I think it's interesting that the role of the sports scientist has become so important at all professional clubs, whether in the Premier League or one of the other divisions. Obviously the higher up the scale you are and the more resources you have as a club, the bigger the department will be. It may have been a very different thing ten or fifteen years ago, but it was something that I could see would help me to do my job. And from a player's point of view, they quickly began to realise not only that their personal performances could be enhanced but that they might be able to extend their careers by a couple of years, which financially can be massive for them.

'I've got no doubt that a sports scientist can have an impact with or without the technology,' insists Nick. 'But it's obviously enhanced with it. I know if I went to a League One or Two club I might not have some of the equipment that I have at my disposal with Norwich, but I could have an impact. The big thing for me is that as sports science has evolved, the players have evolved with it. In many respects they are growing up with it.'

ONE OF NICK's colleagues at Norwich is Steve Rigby, and he too performs a vital role for the club because he is their kit man. If you ask a lot of fans what a kit man does it would probably come down to them saying he lays the shirts out for the players in the dressing room and then collects the kit at the end of a game so that it can be washed. Of course, all of that is true, but there is a lot more to the job – and the sheer logistics of what Steve does these days is very different to the way things were not that many years ago when he started at Leyton Orient in 1998 when he was eighteen years old.

After more than six years with them he went to Charlton, where our paths first crossed, and then he joined me at West Ham before moving on to Norwich. At Orient he would travel to away matches with one or two skips containing everything that was needed for the players. These days he quite literally travels with a truckload of gear that is packed into seven or eight skips, as well as a variety of bags that also make the journey, and it all has to be carefully looked after and cared for by him.

'There's a perception that the players have a new shirt every game, but that's not the case,' explains Steve, 'unless they swap it or it gets damaged. Then it does have to be replaced. At Norwich you might find yourself having to reprint ten shirts, but at West Ham you could be printing fifteen or twenty shirts a game. When it comes to players swapping shirts we cap it at ten. Anything over and above that and it's £60 that the player has to pay, £40 for the shirt and £20 for the name and number. You might be washing the kit and hanging their shirts up, and then suddenly realise that a particular player is missing one. We've got laundry facilities at the training ground and we have a part-time laundry lady who comes in every day to take care of the training kit, but the match kit I predominantly do myself.

'In the summer I go back about two weeks before the players start pre-season training. It gives me time to take delivery of all the new kit, unpack it and sort it out, get the squad lists and apply all the squad numbers and the staff initials. When you consider that there are three sets of kit for all the players – home, away and the third kit – three sets of training kit for each of them and three sets of kit for the staff, you soon realise that you need that fortnight to prepare everything. In the Premier League teams are allowed to wear the same colour shorts as the opposition, but not the same colour shirts and socks. Supporters may think, "Why are we playing in our away kit? There's no clash." But in the week leading up to the game the Premier League will send you a form telling you what colours you're playing in, so there's no confusion any more. There's also a ruling where you're not allowed to wear your away kit more than eight times in a season. We have to tell the Premier League the times we want to change kit, even when we don't have to change it. I'll choose the games, run it past the gaffer, let the secretary know, and the head of retail and commercial will also be involved.

'On a normal training day I'll get in by 6.30 or 7am because a lot of the staff will come in and go to the gym, and they'll use a set of kit and want another set of kit to change into after that. I'll also get the players' kit set out – and in pre-season there'll be two sessions a day, so that means there's got to be two sets of kit. Typically the kit will consist of a T-shirt, shorts, socks, pants, towel, sweat shirt, wet jacket, cycle shorts, ankle socks and long-sleeved under-tops. In winter there will be things like hats and gloves. There's also the 18–21s' kit, the first-team staff and the academy staff.'

In terms of staff at Norwich there's Steve, a second kit man who does the 18–21s, and the laundry lady, but at some other clubs in the Premier League there will be more people involved and there will be at least two first-team kit men. It's a big workload but one that he clearly manages to cope with, and it's a great responsibility knowing that nothing can be allowed to go wrong on match days.

'For a home game I'll tend to go and get it set out on a Friday morning,' he says. 'Then I'll drop the boots off on a Friday afternoon. For away games we travel on a Friday after they've trained in the morning. The team will fly if it's a long-enough journey, but I always travel in the van that we have with all the kit. With the amount of stuff you have to take you really have to go by road. In the skips I'll have the match kit, spare kit, boots, warm-up wear, bench coats, flip-flops, bags, medical gear, fitness gear, drinks, massage tables and footballs. In the Premier League clubs tend to have twenty-four-hour security, so I can set the kit up at the ground the night before. That way if the players want anything or there's a problem you've got the Saturday morning to try to put it right. I then go to the team hotel. Before I came to Norwich I once had an incident where a player left his boots in his car at Stansted Airport. I ended up getting a taxi from the team hotel in Preston back to Stansted, picked the boots up from his car, then got back in the taxi with them and arrived at the hotel at about 5.30 on the morning of the match. That sort of thing wouldn't happen now because all of their boots travel in the skip.

'On the day of the game each player will have their own spot in the dressing room and their own set of kit. They'll have flip-flops, and two shirts hanging up – although some players can't decide whether they'll wear a short-sleeved or long-sleeved shirt, so if that's the case they'll have two of each hanging in their spot. There will be two pairs of shorts, towel, T-shirt, socks, pants, possibly cycle shorts, a long-sleeved under-top and some ankle socks.

'They will warm up in a shirt and shorts. Some players will wear ankle socks, some might have cycle shorts on, a T-shirt, wet shirt and maybe a jacket in colder weather. Then when they come back in they'll take that lot off and put their match kit on, decide on their choice of boots – I'd probably take four pairs for each player – and then they go out for the match. When I was at West Ham I used to have to take twelve pairs of boots to every game for Freddie Ljungberg!

'After the game the lads will bring the kit over to me and it all has to be separated. For home games I'll take it to the training ground after the game and get it washed the next morning; for an away game I'll drive back with it that night, and if we're in on a Sunday the training gear from the previous Friday will get turned around for them to use.'

It's obviously a very different journey for Steve when it comes to away matches than it is for the players. When the match is some distance away and they are flying they will leave the training ground on a Friday, be taken by coach to the airport, fly in their private plane, be met by a coach on the runway at the other end and then be taken to their hotel. After the game the coach takes them back to the airport, they get on their plane, get off at the other end and then a coach will return them to the training ground, where they can collect their cars. Meanwhile, poor old 'Riggers' is on the M6 in his van with a burger and chips!

But on a more serious note, his role within the structure of the club and the first-team setup is very important. For a start, he is privy to a lot of information both from staff and players that is often confidential, he is in and around the dressing room at all times, and he has the trust of management, staff and players alike. He enjoys a good relationship with them all – it has to be that way if he is going to be able to do his job properly.

'It's a great little gig,' he insists, 'but you certainly have to be organised.'

ANOTHER PERSON WHO certainly needs to be organised is a club's player liaison officer. It has become an increasingly important role within the game, particularly with the growing number of foreign players who are now part of our leagues. Mark Maunders performs the role for Fulham, looking after players from seventeen years old upwards, and he has been with the club for eighteen years. During this time he has worked with more than two hundred and fifty players from forty-nine different countries. Some of the bigger clubs might have three or four people performing similar roles to Mark, and the link and services he provides for the players is essential for many clubs now.

'My actual title at Fulham is player care manager,' he explains, 'which is a different way of saying player liaison officer. I think clubs today are not only much more focused on player care and making sure of their welfare, but that of their families as well. It's a welfare role that I perform. So for example, if a player comes to us from Europe he's got to find a house, find a car, get a bank account, sort out a mobile and maybe look for schools for his kids. Some very basic things – they all need taking care of – and that's just the player.

'But what about the families as well? There were a lot of stories from the early Premier League days when players were coming over and they were fine. They came to the training ground every day, they mixed with their teammates and the people around the club, and maybe picked up a bit of English from doing all of that. But their wives were at home feeling alienated – perhaps with a couple of kids in a house that the club had found for them. I think it took a while for it to kick in, but clubs began to realise that it was the wives and families they needed to focus on as well as the players. In those early days I think there were instances where players and their families just didn't settle, and they moved back to the country they'd come over from.

'So what we do with every player that comes to the club, whether it's from abroad or from some other part of Britain, is to sit down with them and do a "needs analysis". This will contain questions like, "Where have you been used to living? Are you used to living in a flat or a house? Do you like living in the country, the city or the suburbs? What's important to you? Do you have any pets? Do you want a big garden, or would you be happier living in an apartment in Chelsea or Fulham?" It's basically asking what their lifestyle is like and how they want to live. We do it with the player, but also with their wife or partner.

'The other thing that's obviously important to a lot of the foreign players is language. If they don't speak English or their English is not very good we'd get them an English teacher straight away – and that would be for both them and their wife or partner. There might also be someone already at the club who speaks the same language as the player who's just arrived, and we would try to get them to work closely with him as well. One of the great things about being a club in London is that the city is so multinational and multicultural, so there's always a community from a player's home country somewhere. For example, the largest South Korean community in the UK is in New Malden, which is about a mile away from our training ground. We signed Seol Ki-hyeon in 2007, but before that he was at Reading and Wolves. When he was in Wolverhampton he was travelling down to New Malden to get his food, so when the opportunity arose to sign for Fulham he jumped at it.

'The players all have my phone number and email, and you can never say how your day is going to be filled. I once got a phone call from a young player who had been living in his apartment for eighteen months. He called because all the electrics had gone out and the washing machine had flooded. So you have to manage the situation on the end of a phone. I got him to mop things up and then told him to go through to the airing cupboard because I knew he needed to pull the power switch back up. The washing machine had tripped and it had kicked all the electrics out.

'I had another experienced player who was an international and had played in World Cups call me over one evening. He'd moved into a house and had invited his family and agent over for a meal – but his cooker wasn't working. I popped in on my way home from work to have a look, and when I went over to the power switch on the wall I realised it just needed turning on! I've been in a pub with friends and got a call that meant I had to spend half an hour on the phone trying to arrange for a player's tyre to be repaired. I also had a call from the lost property office at Victoria Station one summer's afternoon telling me they had a Fulham player with them who had left his bag with all of his possessions – including wallet, phone, keys and passport – on the Tube. So I had to drive into town, get some cash for him, arrange for a locksmith, cancel all of his credit cards and start making phone calls to deal with all the other stuff that he'd lost.

'Sometimes my mates will say, "Why don't you tell them to do it for themselves?" and I explain to them that's why they couldn't do my job. You have to have a level of patience and care for people in order to do it properly. You do get different personalities as well who have different levels of self-reliance. So one player may be very independent – you'll have one or two conversations with him, then he'll go away and start making appointments for himself and start organising things. But another guy will come in and see you every day and ask you to do things for him. Sometimes you have to be firm and say, "Look, I'm not going to do this for you. But this is how you do it." You do get an attachment to people, but overnight they can be gone because they get transferred, and then you have to manage them out of the business as well. So when they move you make sure things like a house sale goes smoothly, and that things like utilities are cancelled. It's not just the first-team players who get looked after, either. There are also managers and coaches who might need help when they come in.

'When it comes to the young players there's an educational process as well, which we call "A Professional Life

Plan". It includes looking at their aspirations and then giving them practical advice on all the things they need along the way. So we'll put on sessions on money management, and on things like cooking and knowing how to work all their domestic appliances and where all their important facilities are. The young lads who have come through our academy are very rounded individuals.

'I'm employed by the club and my priority, whatever happens, is to Fulham Football Club. The two owners who I've worked with have both invested a lot of money in players, and it's my job to make sure that when these players go out training or when they go out to play a match they're as focused on that as they can be. You certainly have to be a jack of all trades. You've got to have the right personality and you've got to be unselfish. It can play havoc with relationships. But in the end you like to think you've played your part, no matter how small.'

I think the role that Mark and others like him have at clubs is vitally important, because they are an integral part of making sure the players are getting the opportunity to give their best for the team. The manager might know more about the player as a footballer, but I wouldn't mind betting that the player liaison officer or the player care manager knows more about a player as a person.

CHAPTER 10

FA

Greg Dyke

IN THE SUMMER of 2013, after about a month in his new job as chairman of the FA, Greg Dyke sat at his laptop and created a new file.

'It was titled "FA – Early Impressions",' he recalls. 'I wanted to note down my thoughts about what I'd seen and what I believed needed doing. It's an organisation that doesn't like change much, but it had to be changed – and that's what we've been doing. Back then what really struck me was that the FA had an image problem and that there wasn't enough thinking being done, because everyone was busy doing something. So what I was saying was, "What do we actually want to do? What's the aim?" Which is what you do in any business. It was about saying, "What do we want and what are we trying to achieve? We want to do that, that, that and that – so let's do those things and forget about this, this, this and this." It was then about working out a strategy, and we've since changed a lot of stuff. If you're going to change the strategy – and change where you're going – you've probably got to change the people. And that's what we did, although it doesn't make you terribly popular with some people.

'There were – and are – things being done just because they've always been done. For instance, I discovered one morning that the FA gives a grant to Oxford and Cambridge universities – but they've got all the money in the world! They're very rich universities. So let's give the grant to poor universities. It's those sorts of things, and that tells you the whole story. We've got a really good chief executive now, Martin Glenn, who came from the service industry. The FA spent years saying, "We're the FA." But you've got to ask, "Who do we serve? What are we trying to do?"

'Modernising this place is a struggle. Not with the staff – because the staff are great – but with the structure, and the FA gets judged most of all on whether or not England win football matches. In the end we've got to start winning some tournaments. I've got a maximum of four years here, then I hit seventy and I'm out. You can move an organisation forward in that time. In commercial organisations you do it all the time in three or four years. What you do is put in a management structure and a management team.'

It seems that Greg has identified some key areas that he thinks the FA should be concentrating on. There is obviously the national team, but there are also things like the need to bring young English players through to play at the highest level of the game, producing coaches for the professional game and for grassroots level, and providing facilities for kids and anyone else who wants to play football.

'That's all you can do, and what you should do in any business, any organisation,' he says. 'Ask what you're trying to achieve. You can't do everything – and you've only got so much money – so you want to spend your money where you think it matters. And you've got to take the board and everyone along with you.

'Part of the structure was that we want to do all that we can to get more English kids through the system, but that's hard because the clubs are pretty reluctant. It's my bugbear with English football – the figures are pretty horrible. I was shown some figures that said over 70 per cent of kids who sign as a scholar at sixteen years old are out of the game by the time they're twenty. These aren't any old kids – these are the talented kids who have been identified as such when they were young.

'We've got a real issue in this country. In the past you'd play in youth teams, the reserve team and then get into the first team. In the course of doing that you'd get to play against and with some old professionals. That doesn't happen now. All that the kids do is play against each other on training grounds for years. I spoke to an Under-21 coach at a Premier League club and he said that they can play up to three over-age players, but he said he'd change that rule to say that you've *got* to play three over-age players. So I came up with this plan to try to get B teams in lower leagues. But I couldn't get the lower leagues to agree, and that's one of the frustrations of the job – you know what should be done, and you can't get it done.

'Most weekends in the Premier League fewer than 30 per cent of the players are English, and if you look at English players who are in the Champions League the figure is lower than the Germans, the French and the Spanish. You're probably down to about 20 per cent. We've got a real issue with English players coming through. There's the view that if kids are not good enough at the age of ten then they're never going to be good enough, and there's the other view that there are some good kids coming through but they don't get beyond the Championship. No one objects to clubs bringing in top foreign players, but there are a lot of very average foreign players out there.

'When we got the Bosman ruling in 1995 everyone said it freed up players, which is true. But what it also did was that under European law you could no longer say that you can only have English players. That was a disaster for English football, because it came at the same time so much extra money went into the game and you could buy in Europe. One of the great ironies to me is that some of the clubs with the best youth structures are the ones who are least likely to play the kids. We can try to push and encourage having more English players coming through, but we can't really do anything about it. All we're trying to do at the moment is to stop the decline – and there are some signs of that happening.'

One of the other areas Greg and the FA decided to concentrate on was coaching. Lots of people hear about the national football centre at St George's Park when the England team train in preparation for one of their matches, and it is used for all levels of national sides. But it also has a very important role to play in producing coaches and helping them develop. It's about bringing coaches through, educating them and getting them qualified. A minority of them end up in the professional game, but there are others who will go on to coach in youth clubs and schools.

If I could wave a magic wand now I would make it compulsory for every school to have a qualified football coach on their staff, so that at six, seven and eight, kids could be identified as having talent in primary schools, and all the kids – no matter how good they are – would benefit from being coached football by a properly qualified person. It has to be the way forward for coaching in this country. Not every coach can work in the professional game, but the hope is that good coaches will filter down the system and kids will be better off for it. So St George's Park isn't just about the national team and the other squads – it's also very much about producing a new generation of coaches, although this process takes both time and money for anyone who wants to get their qualifications.

'They all pay, but we've now got a programme where we help some people who can't afford it – because it's quite expensive if you've got to take two weeks off and you've got to pay,' explains Greg. 'So we've now got a programme to offer encouragement to people from different backgrounds, to get more women involved and certainly to get more ethnic minorities to go into coaching. You want more coaches and better coaches. I suspect there are good coaches who've done one or two badges and don't do any more, so we've now got ways of encouraging them, ways to help and assist them if they can't afford it.

'I visited a school in Birmingham that is helping kids to try to become coaches. These kids are not going to go to university, so they spend two years learning to be coaches and in the third year they go out into a primary school, where most of them have now got jobs as teaching assistants. It's changing. My wife's sister was a primary school teacher – she turned up one year and even though she didn't know what a football was they put her in charge of football!

'So we've re-organised and there's now someone in charge of coach education, because what was happening was that someone would get Grade One or Grade Two and they never heard from us again. But now with today's communications, you can keep in touch with anybody.'

Having decent facilities to play football is another big part of what Greg wants the FA to do. It obviously encourages not only kids to get out and play, but also a whole range of people both young and old who want to play and be involved in the sport.

'We've got a pilot scheme in Sheffield where we're trying to examine the whole need for grassroots facilities,' he explains. 'We look at things like more all-weather pitches and other things that they feel they might need, and then if it works we'll gradually roll it out across the country. An all-weather pitch costs you about £1 million – we get the local authorities to put in a third and we find the rest. We got the government to give us some extra money because the secretary of state asked me after the last World Cup in Brazil, "What do we do to give you a better chance next time? I'd like to set up a task force, a committee." I said we don't need another committee, just spend some money on various different things, and I told him what they should be. They gave us £10 million a year for five years, some of which is used on coaching and some of which is used on facilities.'

Greg's career has seen him take charge of some big organisations in the past, including being chief executive at both London Weekend Television and Channel 5, as well as being the BBC's director general. His links with the world of football go back a long way, including sitting on the board of Manchester United and being chairman of Brentford. When he was at LWT in the early 1990s he hosted a dinner for the chairmen of the so-called 'Big Five' – Manchester United, Liverpool, Everton, Tottenham and Arsenal – at which the possibility of a breakaway league was discussed. This would eventually see them and other top clubs in what was then the First Division break away from the Football League in 1992 and form a new league. When the initial decision was made to break away they went to the FA and got their seal of approval for the idea, which eventually became the FA Premier League, although it seems that the FA missed out on the chance to cash in on what has now become a worldwide product.

'There was a moment,' reveals Greg. 'I was involved when they set up the Premier League. I was running LWT at the time and I hosted the dinner where the "Big Five" chairmen said, "We're out." The most interesting thing at that moment was that they went to the FA to get their permission. If the FA had said no, they wouldn't have done it. But because the FA was waging one of its historic battles with the Football League at the time they said yes. The FA could have asked for anything – and they'd have got it. They could have asked for 5 per cent of the television money, they could have said they wanted the new league to consist of sixteen or eighteen clubs instead of the twenty-two they originally started off with. They could have asked for anything – and they would have got it. That was the one moment the FA had. There's been historic aggro between the FA, the Football League and the Premier League, but we've got to try to calm that down and work with that.'

It strikes me that being chairman of the FA is not the easiest job in the world, although some fans might think it is. A lot depends on what you want to do while you're at the helm for that relatively short period, and Greg has clearly targeted some key areas where he thinks he can make a difference and move things on. So what would be his hopes and fears for the future of the English game in, say, ten years' time, apart from the obvious one of wanting to see an England team winning tournaments?

'I hope that if you're a ten-year-old kid you're going out there playing on decent facilities and that you've got a decent coach – not just the kids who are going to be professionals, but ordinary kids who enjoy playing the game. And I hope we've got more people playing the game – men, women, boys, girls. My fear is that in ten years' time you might find that only 15 per cent of the Premier League are English players. We've got to try to stop that because I think it's unfair on the kids. It's always been difficult for anyone to come through and play at the top. In years gone by it might have been one kid in fifty or a hundred. Now it's more like one out of a thousand.'

CHAPTER 11

MEDIA

Jonathan Pearce, Nick Moody, Andy Cairns

LIKE SO MANY other things in the modern game the role of the media has grown enormously. When I started playing, the media was pretty much confined to newspapers, television and radio. There wasn't any internet, so there weren't things like websites, Twitter or Facebook, and there certainly weren't dedicated sports channels with football matches being seen live on a regular basis. A football fan these days can access matches from around the world and get information about the game at the touch of a button or the click of a mouse. It's a very different world, and the media has had to adapt and move on in order to keep pace with these changes.

But despite all the choice now available to the football fan, there is something that is as important to a young kid today as it was to a youngster more than fifty years ago – the

Saturday-night ritual of sitting down and watching *Match of the Day*. The programme itself has evolved over the years, but just hearing the first few bars of the theme music immediately means something to most fans. When she was young my wife and her sisters used to do a little dance when they heard the music, and in only my second game for West Ham I was interviewed on the pitch after the match at Upton Park by the late Jimmy Hill, who presented the programme for some time. The show has had some very familiar voices commentating on matches, from Kenneth Wolstenholme through to the likes of Barry Davies and John Motson, and for the last twelve years Jonathan Pearce has been part of that illustrious list.

I've known Jonathan for many years, having first come across him when he brought his distinctive style of commentating to Capital Radio as a regular on the London circuit covering games. He went on to commentate for Channel 5 and then at the BBC with Radio 5 Live, before concentrating on television commentary with them for *Match of the Day* and various international tournaments such as the World Cup and the Euros.

The average fan will sit in front of their TV screens on a Saturday night and watch the Premier League highlights on *Match of the Day* without thinking too much about the work and preparation that go into each game. The highlights of a match may only last for six, seven or eight minutes, but it's not a case of the commentator just turning up and muttering a few well-worn phrases and describing the goals or controversial incidents.

'I will always get to a game three hours beforehand,' says Jonathan. 'I'll go through all the newspapers and then try to speak to the manager – he might give me a couple of clues as to how they're going to play and how he thinks the other team is going to play. I'll then do my abbreviated team sheet with all the facts and stats on it, and get that into my head. If I can get any of the players or speak to the players as they come in I will, and then I'll have a chat with the journalists who are at the game. We get the team news confirmed an hour and a quarter before kick-off, and once I get this I'll get up onto the gantry and make sure my position is decent. It's little things, little housekeeping things that you do. You have two monitors, and you want to make sure they're in the right place for you and that generally you're comfortable. The facilities have improved massively and there are fewer gantries where you have to climb up on the roof, although you still do at Everton, up and over a vertical ladder.

'When the match starts you have to have split vision, really, because you're commentating on what's happening out there on the pitch and looking at everything around you as well – the crowd, the whole thing in the stadium. So you've got to train your peripheral vision. There might suddenly be a close-up of the manager on my screen, so I'll make sure I talk about it. There's nothing worse, especially if it's a live TV game, when they do a close-up and you don't mention it. You've got to be aware and work it in to the commentary. Even if they've mistakenly gone to the close-up and there's something dramatic happening on the pitch, you've still got to throw in a line that would link both of them.

'At weekends the agreement is the BBC furnish so many games and Sky furnish so many games. This means that some will be BBC productions and some that I commentate on will be Sky productions. Normally you've got a "talk-back" button, so if it's a BBC production game I talk to the director and maybe say, "Give me a shot of the manager or a particular player who's missed from six yards out." You call the shots and you're more in control. But if it's a Sky production I can't even talk to the director. You can hear him talking to his people but you can't hear them. So, for example, when Gary Neville was doing the co-commentary for them he was very proactive and very good at it. He'd call the shots but I couldn't hear him. So I'm doing my commentary, and all of a sudden they'll go to a shot of a player that he's asked for, and I'm thinking, "What have I missed here?" It's quite unnerving, actually.

'There's also a different style of commentary for a highlights show like *Match of the Day* compared with when you're doing a live game. When you're commentating for an edit, like *Match of the Day*, and someone's had a chance, you'll have to break off your sentence quite rapidly so they can get the cut in. Whereas if it's live you'd normally carry on going, and then I might ask a question to the co-commentator, who I wouldn't have with me if I was doing *Match of the Day*. But you don't commentate in chunks if it's an edit – you do it as if the whole thing is going out. You don't know how long the edit's going to be. People think we commentate on seven or eight minutes, but we commentate on the whole ninety minutes as if it was a live game, although you are conscious that you have to truncate phrases and sentences.

'You also commentate in a different way if you have a co-commentator. If you're on your own it's up to you to describe the action, up to you to call it and also to explain the tactics and replays to the best of your ability. Whereas with a co-commentator who's a player, ex-player or manager, you defer to his superior knowledge. One of the best I've ever worked with is Mark Lawrenson. He'd turn up and ask if you had a piece of paper and a pen, and he might even use the back of an envelope or a napkin to take the formations. You'd look at him and think, "Is he all right? Has he done the preparation?" But it was all done. It was all in his head and he didn't need any notes.'

Jonathan has commentated on more than 2,000 matches during his career in radio and television, covering games at all levels of the domestic leagues and cups, as well as at international events like World Cups and European Championships. For quite a few years the great Bobby Moore worked alongside him on the radio doing co-commentary, and it is one of the matches they covered at the World Cup in 1990 that provides Jonathan with the highlight of his commentating career.

'It was the semi-final in Turin when England lost to West Germany on penalties,' he recalls. 'It was a terrific game of football, and at the end of it Bobby Moore was in tears – it still meant that much to him. We walked back after the game and in the main square there was a mass fight going on. I said to him, "Bob, we can't go through that lot," but he said, "No, we'll be all right." And it was like the parting of the Red Sea! They were all looking at him and saying, "It's Bobby Moore ..." I was tucked in right behind him, and they all got out of the way for us. Then as soon as we'd gone through they all started fighting again behind us.'

The World Cup also presented him with another unusual moment, but this time it was before the finals of the tournament even took place.

'It was in 2006 and I was doing my research for the finals,' he says. 'One of the teams who were going to be playing was Iran, but I knew nothing about them. So I started trying to find out about their players and began researching all sorts of websites to get some information. I spent ages doing it, and one day there was a knock at my door at home and there were some policemen standing there. Apparently all my activity looking at various websites to do with Iran and the Middle East had caused a bit of concern because they didn't know why I'd been doing it. When I told them that I was a commentator and was just trying to do some research for the World Cup, we all had a laugh about it and they even came in for a cup of tea!'

Match of the Day is woven into the footballing fabric of this country, and nobody appreciates that more than Jonathan, who is clearly thrilled to be part of such an iconic show.

'I never ever forget that I'm working for *Match of the Day*,' he insists. 'I never forget that I'm working for the flagship programme of BBC football, and I'm very conscious of the responsibility. To be allowed into people's houses on a Saturday night is very special. I'm working on a programme that is part of the fabric of our society. It's like a constant in people's lives.'

FROM A PROGRAMME that everyone in this country has heard about to a television station that is virtually unknown here but which delivers live Premier League games into around 730 million homes worldwide. I'm talking about Premier League Productions, which operate a year-round Premier League TV channel that distributes 380 live games annually. They produce seven magazine programmes a week, and for the next three years their output will help bring in around £3 billion to the Premier League from the sale of their overseas television rights. They are based near Heathrow Airport in state-of-the-art studios, and their content is as professional and sleek as anything you will see in this country. The great irony is that because they cater solely for overseas customers, nothing they produce is ever seen in this country.

'I think it's the best-kept secret in British TV broadcasting,' says Nick Moody, who is head of Premier League Productions. 'What we produce, what we turn around and what we offer is as good as any other broadcaster in the UK – and better than a lot of broadcasters abroad. It's really professional, but we know we have to keep pushing.'

Premier League Productions is a division of IMG and have been the Premier League's production partner for eighteen years, distributing global overseas rights to the league. During that time the countries and number of people the games reach have massively increased, as has the money that the Premier League makes from overseas sales. As a consequence of this the twenty clubs in the Premier League have also benefitted. When it comes to the money made from domestic TV, 50 per cent of it is distributed among the clubs, 25 per cent is distributed depending on where clubs finish in the league and the remaining 25 per cent is distributed depending on their live TV match appearances. When it comes to the money from overseas it's a straight split between the clubs, and in my view is the major reason why the Premier League is so competitive. With the huge figures now involved the importance of Premier League Productions is obvious.

There is a massive appetite for the Premier League around the world, and the numbers – whether it's the viewing figures, the countries it reaches or the money it generates – are quite staggering. Having worked for Premier League Productions on some of their shows I have been able to see at first hand just how smooth their operation is and the quality of programmes they produce. They produce a channel that can be seen overseas by any country that subscribes and wants to take it. There are also some countries that take the content, or some of it, but have their own studio and presenters. So, for example, NBC in the States will take the live games from the host providers – Sky, BT Sport and the BBC – but they will then use their own commentators, have a studio programme based around the matches with their own pundits talking about the game, while another country might just want to use everything that the people at Premier League Productions put out.

'The operation is split, really,' explains Nick. 'We have the core side to the business, which is basically taking pictures from the host broadcasters, and then there is the content service. We call it a content service and not a channel for a very good reason. We do six and a half hours of live studio programmes every day, and then, looking ahead to whatever the weekend is, we'll screen classic matches between teams who will be playing. This is so a broadcaster can either put them into their own channel or simply broadcast them straight to air. We also send a script so that they can translate it into their own language, if necessary. We even provide clips that will fill the four-minute commercial breaks, or they can populate these breaks with their own commercials.

'When it comes to matches any licensee can take the package, and if they haven't got the funds of an NBC in the States they can just put that game to air. We're constantly thinking of how we can make things better for everyone overseas. Content is king, and we're constantly thinking of how we can give people extra. All NBC ever say to us is, "We love what you gave us. We just want more!" We have a multi-angle replay system – or MARS as we call it – and things like a dedicated wide-angle at matches, as well as a clips service. We also have a show called *Fanzone*, where you will get supporters from all over the world talking to other supporters about their clubs.

'The operation has grown a lot. We have 130 people working here, and that can go up to 175 or 200 at the weekend. We also have a third department within the organisation called Broadcast Services, and they will book all the facilities for foreign broadcasters who want to come over here, be at the matches and do their own bits from the grounds. One of the other things we're looking at is called Digital Advertising Replacement Technology, which would give us the ability for all the billboards around grounds to be replaced with specific advertising for the market the game goes into. So, for example, clubs would be able to say, "Right, in Europe we want the billboards to say this." In the stadium you would see one thing, but in certain markets in the world we would be able to change what is shown on those same billboards.'

The appetite for Premier League games is amazing – even ten years ago I remember arriving in Singapore late at night and watching three live games from the Premier League, one after another. From a club's point of view it's not only the equal way in which the overseas money is distributed that is important and beneficial. The fact that they are seen around the world on a regular basis is also a very big thing. If clubs want to grow their brand and reach parts of the world they would otherwise be unable to, it can only be a plus for them, and I think they are becoming increasingly aware of just how important television exposure overseas is to them.

'None of the clubs are dealing with just a British market,' adds Nick, 'and that is why Premier League Productions is so important.'

That fact was really brought home to me a few years ago on the night Manchester United secured their thirteenth Premier League title with a 3–0 home win against Aston Villa. I was doing some work for Premier League Productions and was asked if I could put in a call to Sir Alex Ferguson to see if we could get a few minutes with him before the game started. I travelled up to Manchester with John Dykes, who was going to be doing the interview, but when we got there we were told that we wouldn't be able to do it because we were not one of the host broadcasters. I had a word with Alex and told him that the couple of minutes John wanted to have with him would be seen by about 750 million people around the world. He immediately got it and said that he'd do the interview, and just as we were talking one of the Glazer family walked into the office. Sir Alex immediately told him that the game was going to be watched by 750 million people, and I'm sure he was impressed by the size of the audience as well.

John's question that night was excellent, because it not only summed up what United and that match meant, it also showed the global reach and appeal of the Premier League. He asked, 'Sir Alex, there's Manchester United fans all around the world who are either staying up, or getting up to watch this game. What have you got to say to them?' Alex said they were going to win the Premier League for them. Manchester United are a massive club and a worldwide brand, but that night also made me realise just how big the Premier League product is. People all around the world love it. They love the pace, passion and skill of the players, they love the crowds and the atmosphere of packed grounds, and they love the unpredictability of the matches.

'What's incredibly rewarding is that other leagues recognise the job Premier League Productions do for the Premier League,' says Nick. 'The league spends millions of pounds with IMG, and it has to be cost effective for them. They have to get a return on their investment.'

That return seems to be getting bigger and bigger with every new TV deal.

THE WAY IN which people get their sports news in this country has changed dramatically. We take a lot of things for granted these days and forget how different they were in the media only a relatively short time ago. It might seem incredible now, but twenty years ago Sky Sports News was just a pipedream in the mind of Andy Cairns. By 1998 the channel had been launched, and today it is very much part of the sporting media. Walk into any football club's training ground up and down the country and the chances are that they will have Sky Sports News on in the background. And for so many football fans the channel's transfer-deadline-day coverage has become a must-see event.

Andy is the executive editor of Sky Sports News, overseeing Sky Sports News HQ, the sports news bulletins on Sky News and the sports news stories that go onto Sky's digital platform. His enthusiasm and drive have been a big part of ensuring that the idea of a rolling sports news channel not only took off, but continued to grow during the eighteen years since its launch.

'The job's invigorating,' he insists. 'You're always challenging yourself, and it's a real privilege. When we started a lot of people said, "There's not enough sports news. You'll never fill it, it'll never catch on, it'll never work," but of course, sports news has exploded. On the back of that, newspapers started doing pull-outs and supplements, then along came TalkSport radio, websites were springing up all over the place and in the time we've been going it's just grown and grown. So it was the right time – and technology enabled us to do it as we were able to get news back so quickly.

'I worked to a three-year plan. In the first year I wanted to make sure we were accurate and built an audience where people could see or hear things that they couldn't see anywhere else. For the second year I wanted us to start breaking stories, beating 5 Live and beating the Press Association, and in the third year it was about once we'd broken a story how did we develop it and take it somewhere further. We are always thinking about where we need to be in three or five years. You've got to be something that's interesting to a viewer every day.

'We work very hard on a conversational style of delivery. Traditionally, a lot of news programmes were someone talking at you, so we wanted a style that brought the viewer into the conversation, which is why people like Jim White might suddenly say, "Hey, listen to this!" It's as if you bumped into a friend in the pub and they've got something to tell you. So that's something we work hard on. When it comes to our presenters we want them to be warm and engaging – we don't want people who look bored, but at the same time we don't want them to be over the top. Our presenters have to be knowledgeable, and all of them are qualified journalists. So we want that enthusiasm, that spark, that knowledge, that authority and that passion. It's really important, and it's got to feel like a conversation and that the viewer is part of that conversation.

'Our presenters also interview, and it's different to interviewing someone on the radio when you can be looking at your notes or preparing the next question while the person is giving an answer. Eye contact is very important for us, and the presenter will be briefed by a team of planners if there's time. It's about how to draw out the best answers, and there are different techniques. We do a lot of training on interviewing and getting the presenters to be really tight with their questions.

'The number of journalists has doubled since we first started, but then we use a lot of freelance people as well – contract cameramen, support staff in the gallery, the technical people in the gallery. So for each programme there's probably about a dozen production staff and probably another six or seven technical staff. But we've also got reporters based around the country. We cover twenty to twenty-five stories a day, with camera crews and reports to feed into that. Television is all about teamwork – and you can't just look at the journalistic team. We rely on the graphics team, we need our marketing team to make sure they market the channel, and we have to liaise with our advertising and scheduling teams. There are so many people involved and it's ever so complex. Everyone has to know their role.

'Journalistically, I realised about four or five years into this whole thing that the traditional training grounds of newspapers and radio were not turning out the people we needed. So we spoke to the training providers – the National Council for the Training of Journalists and the course providers – and explained this. We explained what we needed and we've worked very closely with the NCTJ and the course providers, the people who run journalism courses across the country. We work very closely with them, identifying the skills we need. So the students are getting value for money on a course, and when they finish they are ready for the workplace.'

Although they cover all sports, there is no doubt that the football fan is able to get an awful lot of up-to-the-minute information about the game and what is going on by watching Sky Sports News, and that is particularly the case on transfer-deadline days.

'The great thing about those days is that if there's nothing happening it's just as interesting to the fans,' says Andy. 'If Arsenal aren't signing a player their fans are sitting there asking, "Why aren't they signing anyone?" and they want to keep watching. It's the same as when there's been talk of a player leaving a club and that club's fans are desperate for him to stay. They watch because they're hoping nothing happens!

'It's strange how it grew – it had a momentum all of its own. It started off with us having this overhead camera and Andy Burton with two phones talking to different agents, and it just grew and grew. As the technology changed we were able to be live at more grounds, and Jim White takes it really seriously and does a lot of work on what he thinks might happen, making calls. But everything we do is co-ordinated when it comes to making calls on deadline day.'

I think the freshness of the channel and the ideas they have come up with since first starting have helped make them a success story, but Andy and the rest of the people who work at Sky in a very competitive industry have to ensure they stay ahead of the game and give the viewers something that will continue to interest them.

'I have a "Future for Sports News" day each year when we look at changes in the way people consume news,' says Andy. 'We look at technology changes, the way people watch news on TV, we look at newspapers, what's happening with websites, and what's growing and what's not in the UK and in the States. Then we look at what's new, who are our rivals and what threats there might be to us. So for example, Twitter – is it going to be a threat? How do we contain that?

'Lots can go wrong. You're not always first to every story, and when that happens it hurts. But we're good at learning from our mistakes. That's the beauty of a rolling-news channel. With a newspaper, if you miss a story you've got to wait twenty-four hours to get it right. If we miss a story we can soon catch up, and everybody knows that we've got to overtake whoever's got that story pretty quickly. We're good at that. We report on the people who are the best in the world at what they do, and that should inspire us to be the best we possibly can.

'I've always said how we tell our story will set us apart from our rivals. The way we tell that story makes us better than everyone else.'

CHAPTER 12

INTERNATIONAL

Roy Hodgson, Chris Coleman

ON 1 JANUARY 2016 Roy Hodgson reached a landmark anniversary in his career. It was exactly forty years to the day since he became a manager for the first time when he took charge of Swedish side Halmstads BK. From that day he has been manager or head coach at fourteen other club sides in a variety of countries, and four national teams, including his current role as the man in charge of England. He took the reins just before Euro 2012 and then successfully plotted qualification campaigns to the World Cup in 2014 and Euro 2016.

He was sixty-four when he got the job, and was respected around the world as a manager and coach. In the months leading up to his eventual appointment there had been intense speculation in the press – and the media in general – that Harry Redknapp would be the man to get the call from the FA, but in the end Roy, who was at West Bromwich Albion at the time, was the man they went for, even though he had serious doubts the opportunity would ever come his way.

'The job had passed me by on a couple of occasions when I'd supposedly been close,' he says. 'I had come to terms with the fact that if it hadn't happened on those couple of occasions it might not happen the next time. I did several interviews when I was asked the classic question, "If you get offered the job would you take it, or is it too hot for you and a bit of a poisoned chalice?" I'd reply that I'm English, and that in my opinion it's the pinnacle of any English coach's dream and ambition. If ever the day comes and England come to me and say they've decided they'd like me to do it, I'll take it.

'So in some respects it was a surprise, although thinking back I was given a few tell-tale hints that I just dismissed, really. Now I can understand that I was under consideration for quite a period of time before the FA went out and made what was at the time a controversial and surprising decision, because Harry Redknapp was being heavily touted. I always knew that my background and what I'd done would compare with anyone, but I didn't know if they'd have the courage to stand up against quite a powerful press influence. But they had the courage to say, "We're the FA. We represent football. You're the press – we can't control you, but you aren't controlling us." So they went for me.'

In 2006, when the FA were looking for a new manager to replace Sven-Göran Eriksson, I was one of the people interviewed for the job that eventually went to Steve McClaren. As part of the interview I was asked about handling big-name players, the press, what I saw as some of the pressures of the job and what I thought was expected of the England manager and team. I was forty-eight years old, I'd been a manager for fifteen years and had enjoyed success with Charlton in getting them promoted and established in the Premier League. I felt pleased and honoured to be considered, and there was no doubt that the thought of managing my country was both exhilarating and daunting at the same time.

The expectation levels in this country are huge, even though we haven't won a major tournament as a nation since the World Cup fifty years ago. The more I think about the job today, the more I'm inclined to believe that international management is much better suited to an older man than I was back in 2006. Not only does it mean you have gained that much more experience as a manager, it also means that perhaps you are better equipped to deal with the change in your working life when you cease to be a club manager with all the day-to-day routines that go with that work pattern. Roy's experience as a coach and manager in many different countries, coupled with the fact that he had already managed three national sides, meant that he went into the job with a great awareness and understanding of what the role involved.

'We're obviously always chasing our tails,' he concedes. 'When I came into the job England hadn't won a tournament for forty-six years. Going into the last World Cup it was forty-eight years and then going into the Euros this year it was fifty years. I think taking on the job it would be a mistake to believe it's not possible, but it would also be a mistake to go into it thinking, "This is going to be fantastic and everything's going to be rosy from now on." You know that the battle is uphill, but I think the battle is uphill for Argentina and Germany and other countries as well. Irrespective of our real chances, football is so big in this country. If a tennis player like Nick Kyrgios wins when he's playing a Djokovic, Federer, Murray or Nadal, and if he were to reach the quarter-final or semi-final, they would say he's playing well. We can't benefit from that really, because the expectations will always be high – they will always be there.

'You've got the pick of all the players in the country. I think the club vs country thing has gone now, I really do. I think all the managers accept the national side as a fact of life and I don't find that they fight it. So you've got a good pick, but that has changed even during the last ten years, because ten years ago I don't think there would have been any chance of a player who wasn't a member of his club team playing for England. I don't think ten years ago anyone who wasn't one of the first names, if not the first name on their team sheet, would have been in the squad.

'I've had to accept that in the last few years somewhere between 25 and 35 per cent of any squad I put together will be players who aren't guaranteed to play for their first team. There's probably somewhere around 28 to 30 per cent of English players starting in the Premier League – that will include players who have retired from playing for England

– and there are some very solid performers. But if we're going to be realistic and accept some of these expectations that England will go on and win a major tournament, we can't do that with players who are just good professionals.

'You can't sling them out against Germany, Brazil or Argentina and say, "There you go, boys. Show you're better than him," because they don't have the wherewithal. With respect, a lot of that percentage – if you went through them – any half-serious football-interested person would dismiss the bulk of them. I think that would leave me with the thirty to forty names I can conjure up each time. Albeit if I go to forty, I've probably got as many as ten players who are under twenty-one and just making their way in the game, with only a handful of Premier League appearances.

'You have to be so unbelievably efficient with the amount of time you've got with the players to get your ideas and philosophy across. With a club side, even if you messed up training for one whole week and you didn't get out of your training what you thought you should have got out of it, there's still another forty-six odd weeks to go. With international teams it used to be a two-week break. The league finished on a Saturday and there were no Sunday games to speak of. So the national teams would meet up on a Monday, they'd play their first game on the Saturday, they'd play a game on the Wednesday and then the players would go back to their clubs. So you had ten full days – or eleven, if you wanted to nick the Sunday as well – whereas now of course Sky don't have the international matches, so they put all the best games on a Sunday.

'We had a situation in the Euro qualifiers where something like 60 per cent of our players were involved in playing matches on the Sunday, so as a result there's no point in meeting up on the Monday. You can do it, but you wouldn't do any work because you've got to give them a day off after playing. So you end up using the Tuesday – that's two days after a game for some of the players. We can't afford to say to some of the players, "Okay, boys, have another recovery day." We have to do some work, but you have to be careful with the work you do because you want them to be fit on the Friday and ready for the game. On the Tuesday you've got to be careful – you can't do a session that I would have done with a club side. That has to wait until Wednesday. On Thursday, the day before the game, you can do a bit, go through your set plays, because there's always work you can do. Then you play Friday, so that puts Saturday out of the question, and you're travelling on the Sunday for the next game. So you have to be very careful what you do and make sure that in those sessions you do have you really put across what you think are going to be the important tactical elements. You have to really make sure you use the video sessions and the work you do in those video sessions with them.

'I made two things crystal clear to the players from the very start. I said that if they were going to be an England player they've got to want to be an England player, and I painted a really black scenario about what it could be like – things like being away from their families for tournaments and all the sacrifices they might have to make. Then I said that if they say, "I'm buying into that" and know all the pitfalls and advantages, then they've got to make sure when they come here that they throw their club hat away when they've got their England hat on, even if their manager's saying, "I want you to do this" when we're saying we want them to do something else.

'For example, we push up more than most teams – and certain players, they come to us and we want them to play too high for their liking. So they want to keep dropping back, but we don't want that. We want them to be higher, because we work on pressurising the ball more vigorously. Little things like that. One of the other things I said was that they had to understand that my time's limited, so don't give me that "You need two days after every game to have a rest," because we can't give it to you. Secondly, there'll be more meetings than you normally have with your club – more requirements for you to look at videos and study the videos and learn more about what we're trying to do tactically – because this is one of my coaching sessions.

'If you ask me, "Is this better than being on the field?" I'll tell you, no, I'd much rather be on the field and do it on the field with you. But I haven't got time to be on the field. So every time we get together the principles are so clear in our mind with this team. The things we've got to get better at, more expert at – they don't change. We don't say, "We've changed our mind. Let's not do that."

Roy may be in his late sixties but he shows no sign of slowing up, and his enthusiasm and passion for the game shine through when you talk to him. He's well aware of the age difference between himself and his players, some of whom are in their late teens or early twenties. It was something he immediately took into consideration when he began to put together his staff after he took charge of the national team.

'As a manager you can only cover certain things really, because many aspects of your personality, the job you've done, the position you've reached automatically divorce you from the group, as does your age,' he admits. 'You can no longer take an interest in their interests. I think what you do is to not try and reach out to them on the terms that would interest them and their peer group. You don't try to have a conversation about the latest films or music, which perhaps you could have done not that many years ago. So you don't try to reach them on that level. But what you do is try even harder to make certain you reach them on the football level, and you make allowances that maybe you wouldn't make quite so much when you were young. I also think it's quite important to have someone working with you who is younger and of that generation.

'When I got the job I knew I wanted Ray Lewington to come with me, firstly because of our close working relationship, secondly because he's a very good football coach, and last because he's a wise football man who I knew I could bounce things off and get good answers from. He wouldn't just be trying to read my mind and tell me what I wanted to hear. He would give me a straight answer, whether I liked it or not. I think it's very, very important not to surround yourself with sycophants, because they might make you feel slightly better but they don't help you do the job.

'After Ray agreed to join me one of the things he and I talked about was the need to get another person on board, and they ideally needed to be someone who was going to be a lot closer to the players' generation – someone who maybe had just finished playing – because that would help us. It would help us get some insights from the dressing room and the playing field, so it should be someone who could relate to them a little bit more and how they were as people.

'We targeted Gary Neville not knowing whether he would join us or not because of his TV work at the time. But luckily he was very keen to do so and he's been a valuable addition. The IT people do a lot in terms of video analysis, talking to the players and getting feedback on what they've been given, getting them to ask questions. They're the same generation as well, and that enables me to step aside to some extent. I don't need to be anything other than important to the players on the training field, coaching the tactics.

'In the last year or so we've made a massive change with the video work we do and we've tried to ensure the players take more responsibility for their part in tactical discussions. So it's not just me standing up and saying, "Right, defensively this is how we're going to play. We're going to hold a high line, the full-backs are going out very quickly to the wings, the centre-backs are going to get across and leave whoever they're marking and trust the fella behind them to get across as well. Midfield players, you're going to be dropping in level with the ball, and when the ball is played back we're all pushing forward ..." Nor do they sit there and go,

"Yeah, okay," with me not really knowing whether they fancy it or whether they're bored with it.

'So we've been using much smaller groups. We get them in, put on videos and say, "Go on then, what do you think? Are you too high or not high enough? Did you push out quickly enough? You tell us what you think." Gary does a lot of the presenting with Ray – I don't do a lot of presenting. Most of my talks these days are more general, but the two of them will spend hours getting the videos together and getting the right clips, because it's very important to get the right clips. A ten-minute clip from a game can take ten hours' work.

'We got the young players to participate in these groups, and also got hold of some of the senior players – three defenders and three attackers. We made clips of two halves of a game, gave it to the six senior players, put them in a room together and said, "You look at this – you know the principles we work on. Come back with any clips that back up what we've been saying, or something you see that you feel is important and that we've not even touched on." We thought they might struggle with it, but we had to break them up after two and a half hours! We asked them if they wanted to present, or if they wanted Gary or Ray to present and they could chip in. They wanted to chip in and let Gary present, and it went really well. They would come in with their points and it had a big effect on the young players.

'With regard to enthusiasm for the job, I think there are two very important qualities in any leadership job – energy and enthusiasm. I still have them, but I also think that all the

matches, all the training sessions, all the meetings and deal-
ings with players that I've had over the years make you a bit
wiser. Wisdom is a really important factor. You're increasing
it all the time, as long as you've got the humility to accept
some of the hard lessons you're learning in life and take
them on board. You can never afford to be complacent or
get too comfortable. Football is not a place for people who
want to be comfortable in their lives. Even when things are
going as well as possible you can be dealt an enormous blow
that forces you into different decisions. Get them wrong and
things can snowball.

'That's the big difference between leadership in football
and leadership in an executive position. An executive is not
as vulnerable as we are to fate and haphazard situations.
They also don't have to deal constantly with a very critical
mass of people – the media, who are looking to pounce on
every misplaced word or gesture. However experienced you
become, however competent you think you are to deal with
situations, you're always being put to the test. People are
always trying to find you out, and complacency can be a
massive danger in the job.

'I also think that having the right mentality is important
– getting your own mentality right, and having an effect on
your staff and getting that right, and the mentality of the
players, who you will be trying hard to influence. In some
respects that can be more difficult, because you're trying to
do it with twenty-five to thirty disparate players who come
from all over the country and vary in age from nineteen to
thirty-four years old. You're going to have a big effect on

their mentality, but that's almost got to come from within the group. The work has got to be done there as an England football team.'

WHILE ROY IS a vastly experienced manager in his sixties with forty years in the job under his belt and has been in charge of four national football teams, when Chris Coleman took over as the manager of Wales in January 2012 he was just forty-one years old, with nine years' experience as a manager. He was thrown in at the deep end in 2003 when he became manager of Fulham in the Premier League, and went on to manage Real Sociedad, Coventry and the Greek side Larissa before taking over as the Welsh national manager from Gary Speed, who died tragically in November 2011.

Chris is a proud Welshman who played as a centre-back for his country, and he was obviously delighted to be appointed as their manager. In 2015 he led his side to their first major international tournament since they competed in the 1958 World Cup, when Wales qualified for Euro 2016 in France. But Chris admits he found it difficult coming to terms with the role when he started.

'If I'm honest I think I struggled with my relationship with the players when I first got the job,' he admits. 'Because they weren't my players – I just borrowed them from their clubs and it was a slow process for me to get my head around. Having had a relationship with players at club level where you're in it every day with them, suddenly I was only seeing them four or five times a year. Sometimes if you only have one game, you'll only have them for two days. It all seemed quite cold and distant, and I don't like working like that. So I struggled greatly with the job initially.

'But then what I did was that I started to go to them, to open up. When we were in camp I'd go to them individually, sit down and have a cup of tea with them – not to talk about what I wanted from them in a game, but to have a laugh and a joke. Ask them what they did at their clubs, talk about their families and generally find out more about them as individuals. That's when we started to get a better bond. That connection between manager and player started getting a bit tighter, and they probably got to know a bit more about me as well. You could almost feel it on the training ground. There was more of a trust and more togetherness.

'The other thing that happened was that I ended up going down a completely different path. In my first twelve months I was doing things that Speeds was doing before me. If you're going to do it your way you have to do what you believe in. If you're telling a player what to do and you don't believe it yourself, they'll know – and that was a problem I had. I was doing something someone else had been doing. It wasn't until I started doing what I wanted to do that the players probably believed in me more, and I was delivering.

'Before we'd kicked a ball I wrote a system down – 3-4-3 – but I didn't have the heart to do it exactly as I wanted to do it, and it was going on and on. But then we completely changed the system, started to talk to the players about what we needed from them individually, and that's when we began to build rapport and trust with them. It was also when the results started to be a bit more positive.

'We've got good players, but Gareth Bale and Aaron Ramsey are our best two players – so the question was, "How do we get our best players in the best positions doing the most damage for us?" We have the 3-4-3 system, but we can tweak it. It can be a very negative defensive formation, but you can switch it the other way and then it becomes super-offensive. The only things that stay the same are the wing-backs and the central defenders – it's the shape in front of them that changes. Sometimes we've gone with two sitters, two number 10s and a striker. Sometimes we've gone with two strikers. It can be flexible. We tried it in training, then we did it in games and we got results. Then everyone starts believing in it.

'It's very different being an international manager to being a club manager, because I've always enjoyed that day-to-day contact with players. It can be a bit lonely after a game – everybody goes, and then there's just you. When you're a club manager everything leads to you and it's all on top of you, but you get used to that. As an international manager, all the staff and all the players go back to their clubs and you're left there to pick the bones out of it. That still gets on my nerves a little bit, especially when you want to talk tactically to someone – but everyone's gone. You get the video, watch the game you've just played, and it's quite tough just sitting there on your own. You've got a game coming up and then after that you maybe don't play for another three months. So win, lose or draw, after the game you know you're not going to get them together again for another three months.

'We video every training session and every match, so about two or three weeks after a game I'll speak to our video-analysis people. We'll put together clips for the players and have them ready for them when they come back before the next game. So good, bad or indifferent, all the points are on the clips – and then when they come back we'll briefly discuss it all. I don't like to have long meetings so it's always about fifteen minutes, but we'll discuss briefly what we'd wanted in training before that game and how we tried to apply it in the game. Did we or didn't we? Then it's on to the next game. But we always make sure we look at the last game, otherwise it's lost. It could have been so long ago and the players just won't remember it.

'The success we had in qualifying for the Euros was fantastic. You get further with a group of people when they're together, when there's good team spirit and good bonding, rather than having a team with great individuals who don't like each other and don't want to work for each other. You get further with a good bunch – and that's what we have. We looked at teams like Croatia and Serbia, and when we played them there was something about their players. It was almost as if they wanted to do more playing for their country. You looked at how many caps some of them had and it was ninety or a hundred. None of our boys have ninety caps.

'So we threw the gauntlet down and said, "Who's going to be the first to ninety?" Speeds had eighty-five caps – the most for an outfield player – but who's going to be the one to top that? We've never had that. Why? Does it mean more to someone else playing for their country than it does to us? So then we said you need to turn up more and when you do turn up there's no such thing as a friendly. Show everybody what it means to play for Wales. Chris Gunter has more than sixty caps and he turns up every game. Gareth Bale turns up from Madrid. Even if he can't play he'll still watch the match. It's a club mentality.

'I played for Wales, and it was the most enjoyable part of my career. So managing them – when you've got the whole nation behind you – that feeling is indescribable. And when the supporters are singing the national anthem that's an amazing feeling. I'm proud and I'm patriotic, so taking it from somewhere when we were losing to taking it some-where we've never been by qualifying for the Euros is fantas-tic. I think it was one of the 1958 boys who was talking about the last time we were in a big tournament. About four of them got off the train in Swansea after they'd been knocked out in the quarter-finals. As they got off a few fans came up to them and said, "All right, lads. Where have you been?" They didn't know where they'd been! But everyone in Wales knew when we'd qualified.

'I enjoy the job and I'm proud to be the manager, but it's definitely got a shelf life for me – and for Wales. There will come a time when somebody needs to come in with fresh ideas, and I'll need a different challenge. But I don't feel like it's that time at the minute.'

CHAPTER 13

FAN

Ray Winstone

RAY WINSTONE IS one of our most successful actors. His performances on both television and the big screen have made him instantly recognisable to millions of people, not just in this country but around the world. He has rubbed shoulders with some of the biggest stars in Hollywood, and his ability as an actor means that he is constantly in demand, so he seems to go from one big movie to the next. Acting is something he loves and is clearly good at, even if it's not always as glamorous as some people may think.

Spending months away from home on location abroad is not always a bundle of laughs, especially for someone like him who loves his family and friends. But when he is in Britain Ray is able to indulge in another of the loves of his life – supporting West Ham United. He's the same age as me – we were youngsters in the 1960s and 1970s – and both of us come from the same area of east London, where support for the Hammers was part of your life when you were growing up.

'When I was a kid it was about your manor, and the main thing about where you came from was the club,' says Ray. 'In a way it was the centre of where you came from, and so I suppose that in a way football was secondary. It was your colours, it was your flag. It's funny because I was never a football hooligan. I would never be the one who turned up on a Saturday and screamed and shouted and had a row. I just liked watching players like Bobby Moore, Geoff Hurst and Martin Peters – all of those guys. Bobby Moore became a kind of hero. After that it was people like Billy Bonds.

In the East End in those days – and to a certain extent south London – the most famous people were the gangsters, the Krays and the Richardsons. Then you got a figure like Bobby Moore who not only played for West Ham, he was also the captain of England. I think he brought a bit of romance and a bit of honour to the East End. It's still something that I hold with me dearly to this day. So I think first and foremost it's been about where I came from with West Ham, and the football has been a secondary thing. I remember being in the middle of the Australian bush making a film, and we were there for three or four months. There weren't any mobile phones or anything like that then, and when you got the newspapers they were two or three days old – but you'd look for the West Ham result. It just reminded you of where you came from.

'I remember that when my mum and dad moved away to north London I didn't really want to move because I had all my mates where I lived. So I guess I became a stronger West Ham fan when I moved away because I yearned to be back there – that was my roots, that was my club. But there's little reason to go back to where I grew up today because everyone I knew there has moved out – or they're banged up!

'My first memories of going to Upton Park was of the noise and the atmosphere. It was electric. It was an evening game under the lights – I think it was against Wolves – and I remember that it was a bit damp. And it was just fantastic! It must have been in the mid-sixties. Then I remember going over there with my mates when I was young. I'd go with a few of the boys and I'd sit on a step that was almost on the side of the South Bank stand behind one of the goals. I can remember being just to the side of the goal one day when Clyde Best hit a shot against the post and the whole goal shook – it went backwards and forwards and seemed to go on for ages. I remember things like Geoff Hurst missing a penalty when Gordon Banks saved his shot in a League Cup semi-final in 1971. I used to love watching Geoff Hurst – his running off the ball and all his little flicks in the air.

'When I was young my dad had a fruit stall, and me and a kid called Billy Brown used to take it in turns to work on the stall on a Saturday. One Saturday I'd work, the next he would, and on the days we didn't work we'd go to West Ham. I loved going but I was never one of those fans who had to have the same routine every time they go – put on the same trousers or go to the pub before every game. I'm not one of those who shouts at the manager, "You don't know what you're doing," although I might have felt it at the time! But I guess I've been in a bit of a privileged position later in life, because I've got to meet the managers and it becomes a bit more personal. I'll sit there sometimes and there'll be someone in front of me jumping about as if their life depends on it, but at the end of the day it's a game of football. Believe me, I do get fed up on a Saturday if we get beat, but it doesn't hang around with me any more.

'It's funny, but as I've got older being a West Ham fan has been like being an optimist. I'm sure it's the same with fans at lots of other clubs. It's the thing of always thinking that next season's going to be a blinder. When we beat Arsenal at the start of last season I'm playing in Europe already! But then you kind of know that we come down with the decorations at Christmas. I sometimes think it's to do with our song. Don't get me wrong, I love "Bubbles", but it's all about something fading away. It's not about marching on to glory and we're going to smash everyone. It's "And like my dreams, they fade and die." It sort of sums West Ham up, but then I suppose that's why I love it in a way. I feel like we're the underdog. I'd hate to be a Manchester United or an Arsenal fan – successful clubs. They have one bad result and they don't stop moaning. I've often said, "They should try being a West Ham fan!"

'Supporting West Ham you appreciate the moment. When we beat Liverpool at Anfield for the first time in over fifty years it was a big thing for me. I remember all the old Liverpool teams of the past, and I've always kind of liked

Liverpool and the way they've played football. I can remember the teams with Dalglish and Souness in them. I remember us playing them in the League Cup Final at Wembley in 1981, and we didn't have a bad side. It went to a replay and we lost. They had great sides back then, so to beat them at Anfield – even if it was in 2015 – meant a great deal.

'A lot has been made of the thing about there being a West Ham way of playing, and when I was growing up it was beautiful to watch. We had the quality players – the Bobby Moores, the Martin Peters and the Geoff Hursts. We could move the ball and the team was built to play football. We had ball players. Today, anyone who's any good and who's a ball player moves on to Arsenal, Manchester United or Manchester City. So I'm lucky because I've seen West Ham playing the West Ham way, or the way that I know from the 1960s and 1970s. If you now played the West Ham way that I knew then, you'd be relegated every season because I know we haven't got the players to play that type of football.'

West Ham have had a reputation over the years for producing good, talented youngsters. But holding on to them, as Ray says, has been difficult. Players want to move on, the money on offer to the club can be huge and the practicalities of professional football life mean that the make-up of the club's teams has changed, particularly in recent years, with more foreign players being bought and less home-grown talent coming through the ranks and reaching the first team.

'It breaks your heart,' says Ray sadly. 'We had players like Frankie Lampard, Joey Cole, Rio Ferdinand, Michael

Carrick and Glen Johnson in recent years. We had an unbelievable midfield of players, class players. When you see those sort of players end up as England internationals, fantastic players with fantastic careers, yeah, it breaks your heart that they went. But they've got twenty years if they play until they're thirty-four or thirty-five, and they've got to make a living. They can earn a lot of money these days if they're good and they've got talent, and we're not in the league of a Manchester United. The money's gone crazy in football and it seems like a lot of teams buy players now just to keep them in the squad. Things have moved on, but I'm a miserable bastard who likes to hang on to the past!

'People want to go and see great footballers playing from anywhere in the world. It's a worldwide thing now and you have to accept that, but I come from the old school, I guess. Personally, I want to go and see a kid from down the road in a West Ham shirt. The Chelsea team that was so successful had Lampard and Terry in it. Arsenal had people like Tony Adams. It meant something to those players – they were Londoners and understood it. How many times have you seen clubs turn up with a foreign line-up in the League Cup or the FA Cup, and with a foreign manager who doesn't quite understand what it means to a team like Cambridge United or whoever, and they turn up thinking they're going to turn them over with a reserve squad, but instead they get done.

'There's something about knowing the history of the club or the game within the country that you're playing in. But I think a lot of the foreign players and managers take a while to understand. I'd like to see the spine – the core of the side – to be players who understand and come from the area. That's when you get the great players like the Stevie Gerrards.

'I've got a great fondness for Bobby Moore – he was beautiful to watch – and there have been others over the years playing for West Ham that I was lucky enough to catch. I've seen some fantastic players, and in the sixties they were probably getting £16 or £17 a week. Now you've got players in the Premier League earning £80,000 a week and more. Football just happens to be in another world today. Can you imagine the money Bobby Moore or Geoff Hurst would have got now? George Best, one of the greatest players I've seen in my life – just think what he would earn. But I have respect for today's players and what it's like for them. They're under so much pressure with the media and everything else. They're like film stars when they're out and about. It's different for them now.'

Ray's fondness for the club and the happy memories he has of watching matches and great footballers – playing for and against West Ham – are the sort of thing every football fan has. Supporters follow their clubs through thick and thin – and for most it's usually thin. I know he tries to get to Upton Park whenever he can, but the last two years have been tough for him as a supporter because he's been out of the country so much with his job. He might not like change when it comes to his club, but at the same time he recognises the need to move on if West Ham are to remain in the Premier League and grow as a club. Their move to the Olympic Stadium will help them do that and increase the crowd capacity at home games by around 25,000, but for Ray and for all West Ham fans it also means having to say goodbye to Upton Park.

'I didn't want to move away from Upton Park,' he admits. 'I don't want to get rid of the past, because the past is what we're all about. It's where we're from and that's probably the last link I have with that area. By moving to a new stadium, if it's run properly it will draw crowds, it will draw cash to the club and it will draw players. But I want to see our youth players come through as well, like Markie Noble did. It goes back to that thing where when I was a kid you'd go and watch West Ham, and you kind of knew a kid who was from a school down the road and who was playing for West Ham. But you've got to look ahead. Football's changed and it's so big now. If I'm away working in the States or somewhere like South Africa there are more live games from the Premier League on television than there are in England. So you've got this big choice of matches, and you can't believe how many games there are and the interest there is all over the world.'

Ray's love of football and of the football team he supports is no different to any other supporter. All fans have their hopes and dreams, and all fans know that whoever they support, the emotions that take hold of them during the course of a game are just the same. Every fan likes to see their team win, but most know the majority of the time they will have to get used to disappointment and seeing their hopes dashed. It's a fact of footballing life for managers, players and fans that only a handful of sides each season are successful in winning something. For others, success can be surviving a relegation battle or making progress in one of the cup competitions. That's the realistic side of the game, but supporting a team for most people is about having those hopes and dreams. So what are Ray's?

'I'd love them to win the FA Cup,' he says without hesitation. 'I'd love to see them win the Premier League in my lifetime as well. We came close to winning the old First Division in 1986, before it became the Premier League six years later, when we finished third behind Everton, who came second, and Liverpool, who won it. We had a good team and came very close with Frank McAvennie and all those boys. But I always love it when we have a cup run. I love the FA Cup – it's always been my favourite competition – so I'd love to see them win it.

'But I think most of all I'd like to see them play football. Go out there and knock the ball around. Not backwards, going forward, being an attacking force and playing great stuff, win, lose or draw. I think that would be the thing I'd most like to see.'

CHAPTER 14

REFEREE

Mark Halsey

BEING A FOOTBALL referee has never been easy. He is the man the fans often love to hate, and he can also get it in the neck from players and managers during the course of a match. These days being a top referee has never been more pressurised, with every decision they make in a game being scrutinised and looked at again and again on television. Since 2001 the referees operating in the Premier League have been professional. They are full-time officials and are familiar faces to any football fan.

Until his retirement in 2013 Mark Halsey was one of those familiar faces and was reckoned to be one of our top referees. He came through the ranks and started as a referee after ending his time as a goalkeeper in non-league football. He was promoted to the Football League in 1996 and a few years later he was taking charge of Premier League matches.

When the elite group of referees was formed in 2001 he, along with twenty-three of his colleagues, became one of that first batch of professional referees.

'I was in Toulon doing a tournament and remember getting a call from Philip Don, who was in charge of the referees at the time, to say that the next season the go-ahead had been given for professional referees, and I was part of that,' recalls Mark. 'I jumped at the chance. It allowed us to train like the players, to do things like going to your hotel early for a midweek game and prepare properly. Before it all came about, if I had a game in Liverpool I would have to get time off, leave at lunchtime, do the game and drive straight back. I'd be home in Hertfordshire at about 3am, and then I'd be up the next morning early to go to work.

'I used to work as a manager at a packing firm, and in the end it got so awkward getting time off that I quit my job and became a self-employed cab driver. So becoming professional allowed us to go up to these games, eat a meal, sleep in the afternoon and arrive for the match having prepared properly. After the game there wasn't a mad dash home, knowing you had to get up and go to work the next day. Instead, you were able to have breakfast in your hotel and then use the gym facilities to do your cool-down. Apart from all the mental concentration you need in order to referee a game there's also the physical side of things, and I'd run between twelve and thirteen kilometres a game.

'It didn't mean that because we were now professional we didn't make any mistakes. Believe it or not, referees are human beings and we all make mistakes. But we did become full-time, and that had to be right when you think that we were operating at the very top of the English game in the Premier League. When it first started we would meet every two weeks. We would arrive on a Wednesday, train hard on the Thursday and then leave on the Friday, which seemed strange to me, because putting in that sort of physical work so close to a game at the weekend didn't make a lot of sense.

'By the time I retired as a referee the get-togethers started on Tuesday lunchtime at St George's. You had meetings and a session where you reviewed and looked at different incidents that had occurred in games. In the afternoon you'd go out and do your running, have more meetings that day and then on the Wednesday there would be some short, sharp training before everyone got changed and left. When we weren't together as a group the sports scientists would give us a programme, and we would have to download the data from the heart monitors we wore when we trained. In the beginning there were twenty-four referees in the elite group and now there are seventeen.'

As a manager I was really pleased when it was announced that there would be a group of professional referees officiating in Premier League games. Managers are judged on results, and we felt that referees should be judged on their performance. Of course it's a difficult job, but having a high level of performance from referees and assistant referees is an important part of the game.

During Mark's time as the man in the middle a lot has changed for our top referees, not least the fact that they now earn around £120,000 a year for doing the job, with some getting more if they officiate in European games, while assistant referees will get around £900 per game. Referees' profiles have never been higher, and all of our top refs are instantly recognisable to football fans up and down the country. They see him for that ninety minutes on a Saturday and quite often will boo him or disagree with his decisions, but they probably have no real idea about what goes on behind the scenes. Like players and managers, referees have to deal with the pressure that goes with the job, and hardly a week goes by without some of their decisions being looked at and analysed by commentators and television pundits. The one thing you can be sure about is that you only really hear about a referee when they've had a bad game.

'That's very true,' says Mark. 'Some referees will lose a game or two because of their mistakes. For me when I was refereeing and cocked up, I wanted to be out there straight away for the next game. It's all about confidence and that first decision in a game. If you get the first decision right, you're on a high. When I was on the elite list I treated every game I was in charge of as my last game. I think I was a half-decent ref, although when I look back now I wonder why I put myself under so much pressure. But that was just the way I was. I tended not to like watching myself on television. I would watch a DVD of a match and watch my positions, and if I made a mistake in the game I would think about how I could rectify it so I didn't do the same thing again. Occasionally I'd watch *Match of the Day* if I'd made a mistake and would sit there hearing the pundits talk about it.

'But you have to move on and look forward to your next game. As long as a referee is consistent within the ninety minutes, it doesn't matter what happened last week in a game, whether it was the match you were involved in or another game that someone else was in charge of. The other thing you have to make sure you do is to manage a game. I would often call a player over after a foul and let him know in no uncertain terms that he'd better not do it again. I'd say to them, "Do that again and I'll nail you!" They knew exactly what I meant, and I never tried to treat them like schoolboys. I think they responded to that, and it helped me to manage the match situation.

'Just like players, managers and coaches, referees have their own routines before and after matches. You're given the game that you'll be in charge of at 4pm on a Monday. I used to get to my hotel at 11am for a weekend game with an afternoon kick-off, and at the hotel you'll have your own little team – the assistant referees – and you might have a cup of tea and chat about the game that's coming up. I wasn't really one for pre-judging players because you referee what's in front of you, but you would chat about who might be playing. I always thought the important thing was never to overreact in a match and to treat each incident separately as it came along.

'Some referees like to do their pre-match instructions in the hotel, but I always liked to do mine at the ground after the team sheets had been handed in. I would go through what I expected of my assistant referees, talking through offside situations, throws, free-kicks, penalties, and who was going to be the "eyes" in certain situations. And then it was really all about the match itself. After the game you'd get back to your room and talk about any key match decisions, and if there had been any in the first forty-five minutes we would talk about them at half-time.

'We never saw any of the incidents again because TVs are banned in the dressing room, and you certainly wouldn't see anything on your phone either, because they have to be switched off. Then twenty or thirty minutes after the game the "delegate" would come into the room. He's the guy who is appointed by the Premier League, an ex-manager, ex-player or ex-administrator in the game, and he will give his analysis of your performance. He'll talk to you about how you did overall, and will then look at things like how you handled the players, your fitness and your key decisions – the big decisions. Someone from the home club will then come in with a DVD of the game and give it to the delegate, who goes away and watches it. Sometimes you might have a delegate who supports you on a decision on the day but then finds he can't support your decision having watched the DVD. He also has to speak to the managers and writes everything down. Later in the week the referee will get all these comments, warts and all. Happily I very rarely got criticised by managers, but if I did and I thought it was right I would agree with what they'd said. But I never held anything against them. You have to accept it and move on.

'There are also "evaluators" when it comes to Premier League games. There are seven assessors, and they look at all the DVDs of Premier League games. They sit and watch them all, and they will look at every single decision that the referee or assistant referee makes. So for example, you might have given a free-kick in, say, the twenty-third minute. The evaluator will look at what you've done and might say, "Yes, he's right, it was a free-kick. But it should have been a yellow card as well for a reckless challenge." They are ex-referees from the Premier League, and you will get their report by email on the Wednesday or Thursday following a match. So the whole process of refereeing a game goes on for a long time because of what happens in the days after a game.

'People might not think so, but it's tough being a referee. You come off the pitch after a game mentally and physically knackered. One lapse in concentration during the match and you can make a crucial mistake that changes everything. In a way a ref is like a goalkeeper. You can be brilliant for eighty-nine minutes, then make one mistake – and everyone remembers it. Refereeing a game is a very intense experience, and you're fully focused. So much so that you never really hear the fans when play is going on. You're oblivious to it all.'

With the introduction of professional referees and the need to produce quality officials, I've often wondered if it might be a good idea for some sort of refereeing academy to be set up, and also whether there might be some kind of fast-tracking initiative to get ex-players involved in becoming match officials, whether at the end of their careers or if they have had to stop playing because of injury. Then perhaps people like Mark Halsey and other former top referees could coach and mentor them as they made the transition from professional player to professional referee.

'I'd love to be involved in something like that,' he admits. 'Realistically, I don't think you'd get Premier League squad players involved, because they're probably multi-millionaires and will want to do other things. But why not look at players in League One or Two? Perhaps the PFA could get involved and tell its members. Then anyone interested could do the exam, maybe get tutored and mentored by someone like myself before being fast-tracked and going straight into something like the National League, and progressing from there.

'So those who want to become referees, fast-track them, just like they do with cricket umpires, where players coming to the end of their careers take a course and go straight into 2nd XI matches to get experience and training. I think we've got far too many referees who are manufactured, and if there was something set up where guys who have been involved in football as players then want to become referees I can only see that as a good thing. You have to keep looking at ways to improve standards and help the game for everyone involved.

'I think having all the officials wired up during a game so that they can communicate well has been really successful, and goal-line technology has been great for the Premier League. I think anything that improves the decision-making process has got to be good, because football is not only a game – it's a business now. There's a hell of a lot of money involved in the Premier League, and that's why it's so important to do everything we can to get the decisions right.

'I think the whole technology thing is going to move on. We've seen it in the States, where it's been used for non-competitive games, and it's been trialled in Holland, where people will sit in a truck outside the ground and watch what is going on during a match and at the decisions being made. I think it can certainly help and could be used for a key decision when a game is stopped. If a player might be sent off or there's a penalty decision – that's when you could go upstairs and ask for a review. How long would something like that take? No more than about ten seconds, so there's no real interruption to the flow of the game, and the big decisions can get looked at.

'When I used to give a penalty I usually knew if it was the right decision because of the reaction of the players. When players started running around you it was often a case of thinking, "Maybe something's not right here." That's when a referee could go upstairs and get advice on what had just happened. They might say, "Yes, it's a penalty," or perhaps say, "No penalty. Caution for simulation." Everybody would be happy, and the crowd would love it as they waited for the verdict. I think it's got to come.'

One of the most common complaints from fans and the media is that we never hear from the referees when they've made big decisions that have had a major effect on a game. They don't come out after a match and explain why they made their decisions. So will that change in this country?

'I think something like that has happened in Australia, where if there are big decisions they have to come out and talk about it,' he says. 'I think it should happen here, but I think it should be the delegate, not the referee, who comes out. He's in control of what's happening, and he's the one who speaks to you about your performance when you sit and talk to him in the dressing room. So all the key decisions will have been discussed and you tell him why you acted in the way you did when you made those decisions. So I think that forty-five minutes after the end of a game he could go in front of the media and explain everything to them.'

I always got on well with Mark. He was a good referee and approachable even when you weren't happy with what had gone on. But there's no doubt that refereeing decisions can often be a contentious issue with managers. So much can depend on just one decision, and in the heat of a match people lose their temper and composure.

'I had a pretty good relationship with managers, but of course things can sometimes get a bit strained,' he admits. 'I remember towards the end of my career I refereed a match between Millwall and Leeds. Neil Warnock was the Leeds manager, and on the day I sent off one of his players. At the end of the game he stopped his players shaking my hand. I was furious. It went in my match report and Neil got fined. We laugh about it now and had a great time when we both worked for BT doing their football coverage a few seasons ago, but feelings do run high. Football is an emotional game, and I also understand how fans get frustrated and angry with referees and officials.

'I'm a fan as well, a massive QPR fan. My uncle used to live just around the corner from the ground so I was brought up supporting them. You have to tell the authorities who you support so that you don't referee their games, but early on in my career I was involved as an official in a few of their games before I actually let them know that I was a Rangers supporter. Of course, I officiated exactly as I should have done on each occasion, but it was a bit of a strange experience. I ran the line at Loftus Road when they were playing Manchester United. Rangers were 1–0 up, and I remember how desperately I wanted the referee to blow his whistle and end the game. On another occasion I actually refereed a game between them and Portsmouth. John Spencer scored for QPR, and all his teammates were jumping on top of him celebrating. I remember thinking how I'd have loved to have joined in! I refereed them once more when they lost to Huddersfield, and then said, "No, I didn't want to referee their games any more."

'I loved the career I had and the people I met doing it. I used to love going to all the grounds, and it was great walking out at places like Anfield and hearing "You'll Never Walk Alone". I also used to like Goodison Park – the fans there really knew their football – and Upton Park was always very atmospheric because the supporters were so close to the pitch. One ground I didn't like was The Valley when I did Charlton matches. Not because I didn't like the place or the Charlton fans. It was more because I never really seemed to have a good game there.

'There is no age limit any more when it comes to having to retire as a referee. As long as you're fit enough and meet all the other criteria in place you can carry on. But although I loved refereeing and had some great times doing it, in my final season I wasn't enjoying it any more. It got to the point where I'd be sitting in the dressing room at half-time thinking that I didn't really want to go out for the second half, and that's when I realised it was time for me to pack up.'

CHAPTER 15

EXECUTIVE DIRECTOR OF FOOTBALL

Les Reed

IN THE SUMMER of 2009 Southampton Football Club found themselves facing a new season in League One with a ten-point deduction. Today they are not only in the Premier League, but are held up as a shining example of a well-run, forward-thinking club that have defied the odds and gone from strength to strength as they have established themselves in the top tier of English football.

It is quite a remarkable story, and at the centre of it all has been a man I know well, who now performs a role that is unique in the Premier League. His name is Les Reed and he is the executive director of football at Southampton. The job he has done has attracted admiring glances from other clubs. They have seen what has been achieved in a short time by a club who are not one of the league's big hitters, but whose careful and thoughtful planning both on and off the pitch means that those dark days of 2009 now seem like a lifetime away.

I've known Les since I was in my late teens and playing for West Ham. He was a regional coach with the FA and I had decided to take my coaching badge. This meant me turning up for six consecutive Sunday-morning sessions – and Les was the coach in charge. I did three, and then on the fourth weekend I got injured playing for West Ham's first team on the Saturday, had to go for treatment the next day and so didn't turn up on the Sunday. When I went to the next session Les was waiting for me. He said just three words – "You have failed." I couldn't believe what he was saying, but he was adamant that because I'd missed one of the sessions I'd failed. That was it! No discussion about why I hadn't been there. He wasn't going to budge.

Despite that unfortunate episode I later got to know Les quite well whenever we encountered each other on various courses I attended, and I knew he was an excellent coach. When I first became a manager in 1991 it was in partnership with Steve Gritt at Charlton, but in 1995 the club decided they wanted me to take sole charge and that meant I had to look for a first-team coach. The man I went for was Les. We were very different in many ways, but we complemented each other well and he spent three years alongside me, culminating with us being promoted to the Premier League following a memorable play-off win at Wembley against Sunderland in 1998.

A few days after that win Les left to rejoin the FA, who he had been working for as regional director of coaching until he came to Charlton. He became director of technical development with them, and then went on to assume the role of technical director before leaving in 2002. After that he acted as a consultant before going back to Charlton in 2006 to become manager Iain Dowie's assistant. Les had a brief spell as Charlton's manager in December of that year, and then went on to coach at Fulham and become their director of football. By the spring of 2010 he was once again acting as a consultant, and it was in that capacity that he was first contacted by Southampton. Les takes up the story.

'I came here on a consultancy basis towards the end of the 2009–10 season. They had come out of administration and the new owner, Markus Liebherr, and the chairman at that time, Nicola Cortese, wanted to know what they needed to build. They wanted to invest in Southampton and turn it into a Premier League club. They were in League One at the time and had a ten-point deduction.

'I started at the bottom end, working through the academy and upwards and putting a plan together. The season finished, I gave them my report and then went off to do other things concerned with my football consultancy work. They called me back later that summer and basically asked me how the plan should be implemented. I thought they were still looking at me as a consultant, but halfway through the conversation it was clear they wanted me to come in and do it. I wasn't sure I wanted to at first but they persuaded me.

'When I'd sat down with the owner he'd had a very clear vision of what he wanted to happen. He wanted to be in the

Premier League within five years, he wanted to be in a position to sustain a place in the top half of the Premier League, and from that he wanted to build a platform from which the club could then get into Europe and start winning trophies. He also wanted the fans to buy into what we were doing as a club and to enjoy coming to games. That meant he wanted the team to play football that they would like, and he was also very clear that he wanted a proper sustainable business plan so that if anything happened to him the club would never go back into administration. That was what I was presented with when I first joined the club.

'I put together a five-year plan which was going to enable us to get to the point that he wanted, and although the owner financed it to enable those things to happen, he didn't throw mega-money at it like Chelsea and Manchester City have. It was always an investment. It was always about how to build the club so that when we got there we could run a business that stood on its own two feet without the owner having to continually bail it out. It was going to be a sustainable club.'

Les joined the club as executive director and head of football development, and he basically began to run everything outside of the first team, who at that time were managed by Alan Pardew. When Southampton parted company with Alan in the summer of 2010 the club were left with the job of finding a new manager who they felt had the potential to move the team on, and that meant gaining promotions if they were going to fulfil their dream of becoming a Premier League club once again.

'What changed at that point in terms of the next manager was that I recruited him,' says Les. 'We essentially started with a blank sheet of paper, and I was very clear about the way it should be done. There had to be a job description, some criteria that we needed any potential manager to buy into, and then we had to interview them properly in a structured way. We had about five people on the shortlist and did the interviews. We were a League One club at the time, and there were three English managers and two foreign coaches on the list. One of the English managers was Nigel Adkins and in the end we picked him. Apart from everything else we were looking for, Nigel had got two promotions into the Championship with Scunthorpe, so that certainly fitted the bill. But he hadn't experienced the sort of setup we had here. Scunthorpe were a smaller club and he'd been much more hands-on with everything because he'd had to be. When he came here we basically said to him that all you've got to do is coach the team.

'Having recruited Nigel it was agreed he could bring three other staff with him, but everything else – medical, sports science, scouting, recruitment – would be supplied as a service to the first-team manager. He could tap into these as much or as little as he wanted. If he wanted to get heavily involved he could. If not, he could step away from it. Basically, it was all part of us wanting to create stability so that when there's a change at the top, for whatever reason, everything else stays the same – with the culture and philosophy of the club carrying on. My working relationship with Nigel was to say to him I'll make sure everything off the pitch is running smoothly. When you need something, come and see me and we'll make sure it gets done.

'The question was, what do we want the manager to do? Essentially, you want him to pick the team, plan the strategy and coach the players to get the results. So the next question is, what can you put in place so that he focuses entirely on that? The picking of the team bit and the selecting of the squad are where recruitment comes in, and you therefore want your manager to have as much input as he wants or needs. So that comes down to what kind of player do you want, what profile do you need? It comes down to a choice between two players – which one do you want?

'Once the manager has made that decision, all the rest of the hassle that goes along with that they don't have to worry about. So contracts, negotiating with the other club, managing the budget – all those sort of things – they don't have to worry about once he has agreed on the player we're going to go for and he's happy with that. We put some basic rules in place, and during the five years since we appointed Nigel we've refined these. During Nigel's period with us we were still transitioning and fine-tuning everything, but later on the ground rules were set. Obviously promotions, the style of play and the quality of player we needed in League One and Championship level taught us a lot. If we were really going to compete in the Premier League we had to think about what we needed to be doing.'

Southampton's choice of Nigel Adkins as manager proved to be spot on. They gained successive promotions and in the summer of 2012 found themselves back in the top flight, but halfway through that first season in the Premier League a change of manager was made. For lots of people the man who came into the club – Mauricio Pochettino – was a completely unknown quantity, but thanks to the ground rules and systems that were then in place at Southampton he had been very much on the club's radar.

'Part of what we do here is not just to monitor players and their progress,' explains Les. 'I'm always looking at coaches as well. I'm always glancing over my shoulder thinking, "What if?" I have a file in my drawer with names of potential coaches. And it changes. Coaches I might have had in it last year might not be in it this year. When it came to replacing Nigel it wasn't that we wanted to go and get a foreign manager – it was getting someone who would buy into what we wanted. The style of play, using young players, did he have any experience of Europe, was he a coach who could learn about the Premier League and develop?

'There were four or five candidates in the frame, including a couple of English coaches. We were quite interested in Philippe Coutinho at the time. He was a young player with Espanyol and had been on our database since he was about eighteen years old. We'd watched Espanyol a lot, we liked the way they played, and Mauricio was their coach. I did a bit more digging and found out that he had a good track record with young players and bringing them through from the academy. He ticked a lot of the boxes for us, and when we interviewed him he clearly showed that he had the personality, drive and ambition that would fit what we wanted to do. We could say to him that you're the coach, no one's going to interfere with your tactics, how you manage the team on the day or what decision you make. It's all down to you – all the coaching, Monday to Friday. It's down to you and your team of people. But you have to buy into the philosophy of this club.'

Pochettino proved to be a huge success at Southampton. So much so that he became a target for Tottenham in the summer of 2014 after the Saints had finished eighth in the Premier League, with the manager earning praise for the way his team played and performed. But when the Argentinian decided to leave St Mary's for White Hart Lane, Les and the structure he'd put in place at Southampton faced their severest test. Not only did the club lose its manager, they also lost some of their key players. So they didn't just have to find a new manager – they had to reconstruct their squad as well. Once again they surprised many people within the game by recruiting the highly regarded Dutchman Ronald Koeman as their manager, before embarking on a summer of transfer activity that saw around twenty-two transactions take place in a very short period over the summer.

'You can't put a structure into a club that only works when things are going well,' insists Les. 'In the summer of 2014 everyone in the world of football thought this club were going to struggle, but it was the structure we had in place that meant that ultimately we didn't. We lost our manager and several players, but it was important that at the start of that season we hit the ground running. We knew what we were doing. We had a structure and we had a plan, and that was the time these were going to be tested – not when we were chasing for Europe. It was important not to panic but to believe in what we had in place, and I knew we would get there.

'We managed to get the thing with Ronald done so much under the radar, and in having him as the manager we've taken it to the next level. Mauricio, with all the qualities he had, was still to win something or have experience of the Champions League or European football. So if we were looking to the next manager – who might be here for three, four, five years – and if our plan was to be ready for European football, who's on the list that's got experience at that level?

'Ronald met more criteria than all the others. He had Ajax and Feyenoord on his CV, where he'd brought young players through, given them their debuts and they'd gone on to be international players. He also had experience of qualifying for and managing in the Champions League, and had the experience of playing in it and winning it himself. One of our targets is that by 2020 we will have a team that is Champions League-ready. You have to be careful about the terminology. It's not that it's going to win the Champions League. What we're saying is that the quality of the squad at that point needs to be ready to take the opportunity if there's the possibility of a spot. We want to be ready.

'I met with Ronald twice and I had no doubts. There were five candidates on the list and two others were interviewed. I think either of the other two would have done all right for us, but Ronald had more of the boxes ticked and you could tell he bought into the philosophy. The other big thing was that he was used to working with sporting directors. As far as he was concerned that was normal.

'When it came to recruitment Ronald didn't bring anyone in that we didn't know about. He wouldn't have brought in anybody who wasn't on our database as potential for us as a player. For instance, Graziano Pellè had long been identified by us because he'd had two great seasons playing for Feyenoord smacking in goals. He came here and has been a great success. Other, bigger clubs might have looked at him and thought, yes, he's done it in the Dutch league but we want someone who's been scoring goals in the German or Italian leagues. So Pellè is a good example of the sort of number 9 we would have on our system – and obviously Ronald knew all about him as well. Dušan Tadic, who also came to us that summer, was another player who had been in our own system since 2010. We'd clarified with Ronald in early meetings what would happen if certain players left the team. He knew all about Tadic, who'd played for FC Twente against Ronald's teams, and he'd seen a lot of him.

'We have a department for the recruitment of players. We talk to Ronald about what he needs and the type of player he wants, and he leaves the recruitment department to discuss possible targets. We then go back to Ronald and ask him if they fit the sort of player he wants and what his preference is.

'The way it works at the club is that we have a non-executive chairman, a chief executive who runs the business, a commercial director, a finance director and me, the executive director of football. So one non-executive chairman and four executive directors – that's the board. Each one of us has a specific expertise and each one of us gets on with what we're good at. If we all do our jobs properly the whole club is run properly. So I need to work with the finance director and chief executive on budgets. I don't need to have to go back and ask whether it's all right if I spend X amount. I know my budget. I know I can spend every penny I get in, and it's up to me how much I spend on wages and how much I use on transfer fees.

'When you sign a player on a five-year contract it impacts on the club's budget in five years' time. During each one of those five years there is another agent's fee instalment going out, another signing-on fee. I make sure I've taken care of things like that and work very closely with the finance director. We run scenarios. So I'll say, "We want to sign this player on these wages – that's the agent's fee, that's the signing-on fee, these are the bonuses. Run that through the system for me and see what the impact is on five years." We've got a clever piece of software that kind of says, "Yes, that works." So if you're going to buy five players and you run that five times, it will start by flagging a warning over the Financial Fair Play Regulations, and then it might say there could be a scare in three years' time in April that will put us below the line. It lets me know those sort of scenarios.

'Our philosophy here – our owner's philosophy – is whatever you make in sponsorship, commercial activity, transfers can all go back in. If a player who is earning £60,000 a week leaves and we bring in someone who is on £40,000 a week, I've got £20,000 a week to play with. So as long as I'm on top of that I don't have to keep going to the chairman or the chief executive to ask, "Can I do it?" That makes life a lot easier in terms of talking to Ronald. I'm not going to get a manager come to me and ask whether the owner can stump up another £20 million. They know from the moment they get the job that we work to a budget, but that we have the freedom within that budget to trade and use that money.

'The other thing is that the manager knows the way we want to play. We want to play it on the floor, play it out from the back, play attractive football – so that always impacts on the sort of player we're going to be bringing in. You have to work on what is going to happen in the next five years. We call them building blocks – we'll take all the contracts, look at when they run out and look at how durable the different players are.

'When it comes to bringing players into the squad our thing now is to see if they are English or foreign, have they played in the Premier League or have the potential to play in the Premier League? But if they're not available – or if there's someone better – we'll go for them. If a player leaves and there's a gap, and there's isn't someone from the academy or there is a player there but he isn't experienced enough, we go for someone else who's been brought up in an academy somewhere else.

'So, for example, Ryan Bertrand – he was a left-back, and we needed a replacement for Luke Shaw, who had gone to Manchester United. Ryan was still young but had been around the block. He'd been in a Premier League academy, had a Champions League medal but still couldn't seem to get in the Chelsea team. We got him for £10 million in January 2015 after having him on loan for six months, and within a month he was in the England team. On the other side of the field, when our right-back, Nathaniel Clyne, went to Liverpool we needed to go the other way in order to replace him. The next one in our academy was an Under-15 player who is good but wasn't ready to step up. We couldn't find the sort of Ryan Bertrand equivalent in England to replace Clyne, so we then looked at who was young, had come through a good academy system, had a good level of experience in Europe and met the profile we had for that position. We went for Cédric Soares. He was twenty-four, a Portuguese international and ticked all the boxes on the checklist of what we wanted.

'Doing your research on a player is very important. We have eight representatives around Europe who are exclusive to us, and they each have their own domains. We've picked people who have the right contacts and networks to do the job, and their role is to scout players and really dig deep to find out about them. But then there comes a point where our chief scout will go and have a look, and the head of recruitment will go, and if necessary I'll go. But to be honest, if they're recommending them then you're nearly there. You do all that homework because you want them to settle in and be right.'

Attention to detail and planning seem to be key factors in what Les and Southampton have done in the past five or six years. To help them analyse players and opposing teams they have some fantastic facilities at their training complex, such as the famous 'Black Box', which is a room with a viewing area. There's a big console desk at the back where the analysts sit, looking at a huge screen at the front of the room. The club have their own piece of software that brings together all the strands of analytical data they need, and it can be chopped up and shown on screen whenever they need it. They even have remote-controlled cameras on all of their training pitches to record any of the sessions and matches that take place on them. The whole setup is impressive.

The man who started the process by buying the club, Markus Liebherr, died in 2010, and his daughter Katharina is now the club's owner, with Ralph Krueger taking over as chairman. Les describes her as the perfect owner, and both she and the chairman allow him and his fellow board members the scope to do their jobs and run the club. There seems to be no interference – just support and encourage-ment for the plan they have in place and the way the club operates. When the words "technical director", "sporting director" or "director of football" are uttered in the game, people often take a sceptical view of exactly what it is they do, and this view is often shared by managers. In Britain they are roles that have still not really caught on. But the Southampton system has clearly been built for the long term and the club are prepared to stick with it even if times get hard and things begin to go wrong for them on the pitch. The structure is in place for good times and bad, with conti-nuity being a big part of what they are about.

I mentioned that a lot of clubs have glanced admiringly at what has happened at St Mary's, but if any of them want to follow in Southampton's footsteps they are going to have to be brave enough and bold enough to almost completely scrap the way they have operated in the past and start again. Southampton were fortunate in a way, because they had a blank sheet of paper when they came out of administration. But the owner also had the foresight and vision needed to take the club forward. They were also fortunate having someone like Les around to help guide the football side of the club. I've no doubt his experience and knowledge of the game not only helped in this respect but have also been an important factor in his relationship with the manager.

'For me it's the biggest advantage I can have,' he admits. 'I've pretty much worked in all the roles I'm now managing in my position at Southampton. If a manager is at a club for ten years or more they're almost a sporting director anyway, because they've got that experience and built the philosophy of the club. They've been part of it for a long time. But most clubs now don't have that luxury, and it doesn't make sense to effectively give the keys to the kingdom to a manager who might be gone in two years.

'I think Premier League clubs have got so big that it's too much for one man to focus on results, training, coaching and manage all the other stuff as well. So I think what we've got at Southampton is a kind of structure and partnership that works. I'm coming at it from a perspective where I've worked with different managers, I've worked in different roles and I've experienced what they experience. So I see my job as being the person who gets the right man in place and then makes sure that I keep him in place for as long as possible. My job is to ensure his job is as easy as it can be, because what I want him to be doing on a Saturday is making the right decisions in his team selection. I want him to be able to manage the game and not be distracted by loads of other stuff.

'Can what has happened at Southampton happen at other clubs? I say that it can, but they have to choose for it to happen. They have to make that decision and stick with it.'

CHAPTER 16

ASSOCIATIONS

Bobby Barnes, Richard Bevan

THE REALISATION THAT your time is up as a player is never an easy moment for any professional footballer. It doesn't matter what sort of level you've played at, that moment is never easy to cope with. It may be that you've had a long and illustrious career at the top, won all sorts of trophies and international honours, and earned a fortune doing so. It may be that you've spent your entire career in the lower leagues without a sniff of a trophy or even a promotion. Or it could be that you're a young kid who has had their career cut short by injury.

Whatever the reason, it never seems like a good time or the right time, and coming to terms with the fact that their career is over can be devastating for many players. Footballers are temperamentally pretty resilient characters – the nature of the business they are involved in means they have to be – but the change in their life that retirement brings can sometimes be a problem for the toughest of individuals, as Bobby Barnes, the PFA deputy chief executive, knows only too well.

'As a player, football is what you do. It's your whole way of life,' he says. 'When I finished I was thirty-four, and what really brought it home to me was the day I had to go to a doctor's surgery. I'd never been to one before. When it comes to being a footballer I've often described it as being institutionalised, because you're told what time to get up, what time to train, what time to eat. In our day they even took your passports off you at the start of the season because clubs felt they couldn't rely on players to look after them themselves. With the exposure and the money that's come to the game in recent years footballers these days aren't just sportsmen – they're now pop stars, rock stars. But it doesn't matter how much money you've got, it doesn't replace the buzz that a player gets, because football is what they are and who they are. It can cause problems for some people, and from anecdotal evidence we've got a divorce rate into 70 per cent for players between the ages of thirty-five and forty.

'We've got different generations within our membership. There are some former players who earned better money than the average man in the street when they played, but it wasn't vastly more, the way it is now. So a lot of players, unless they're playing in the top echelons of the Premier League, they are going to have to do something else when they stop playing, and they haven't got any transferrable skills. It's not just about players who have had a whole career in the game, either. About 85 per cent of kids who come into the game at sixteen as scholars are lost to the game permanently by the time they're twenty-one. The average career for a professional footballer is eight to nine years, if you take into account those who might get injured and those who get released. It's the most competitive industry that I can think of.'

The problem of dealing with something like retirement is only a part of what the Professional Footballers' Association, or PFA, are about. They have been in existence for 109 years and these days have 4,000 members. They operate a 'cradle to the grave' system for their members, which basically means that once players join the PFA they are members for life, and the organisation offers support and help in all sorts of areas, including mental-health issues.

'There are all sorts of things that people might be finding it hard to cope with,' says Bobby. 'We've been working on mental-health issues for some time, and there can be many ways in which people might be finding it hard to cope. The dressing room can be a pretty unforgiving place, and it can sometimes be difficult for players to confide in anybody. We've now got a network of forty-eight counsellors across the country if a player's got a problem and he wants to speak to somebody away from his club. And all of these counsellors are busy.

'Players can have different types of problems during the course of their careers and after they have finished. It doesn't matter whether you're a top player with a big club or a player with a club in League Two – the problems can often be the same. A player can still fall out with his manager, or the manager wants to get rid of the player. Our role is to provide a balance. If a player does something wrong, the punishment has to be proportionate. It's always the player that gets criticised, but it does work both ways. The players are the employees and the clubs are the employers, but we're there to provide a balance – our role is to educate and protect.

'A former player might come to us because he needs an operation on his knees. A member could have had a heart attack and might need a heart bypass operation, or we might have to buy a wheelchair for someone. We pay for funerals and for care in nursing homes. We never turn anyone away at whatever level, be it a Premier League player or someone who was a scholar with a League Two club ten years ago. If you become a member you're always a member – it's something we're very passionate about – and whether you're Wayne Rooney or a lad from Rochdale your subscription is the same, £150 a year. There are things like non-contributory pension benefits, we supply boots and trainers for everyone outside the Premier League, and they get career-ending insurance – we encourage them to take out their own as well. There are also education courses, which have seen lads going on to get their masters. We also had a couple of lads who became commercial pilots and another who became a dog groomer. Our education department is probably our biggest investment. We spend millions a year on different education programmes for members who want to learn a particular skill or trade.

'Everyone talks about the Premier League and the money involved, but what about Leagues One and Two? Contracts have got a lot shorter, and the upper hand is more with the clubs now. There are 600 or 700 players on the disengaged list each year. Contracts have become one year, and so from Christmas onwards you've got lads looking over their shoulder. So our guys are out there saying to them, "What if? If you're not going to be playing, what else would you want to do? What else can you do?"'

Apart from the subscriptions, the vast majority of the money the PFA receive comes from a share in the television revenue that the Premier League, the Football League and the FA get for their broadcasting deals. The PFA have an annual turnover of around £25 million, and this allows them to put different initiatives in place to help their members on all sorts of levels, including trying to educate youngsters about the harsh reality of making it as a professional footballer.

'We try so hard,' says Bobby, 'and our lads will go and speak to them. There may be fifteen kids there, and they'll tell them that statistically the reality is that out of their group one and a half of them will become a player. But all of them think they are going to be part of that one and a half. You'll always get the ones who you know are nailed on to be professionals, the ones who will go on and have a great career unless they have a serious injury. But you have to look into the eyes of all those kids and tell them the reality of what they're trying to do.

'Another problem for young players can be the money. Players these days are so sought after that the money they get is far in excess of what they've actually achieved. All of a sudden you get kids who haven't done anything – and may never do anything – on big salaries. If a player gets a Premier League contract it's very difficult for them to say, "I'm going to play in League One or League Two – I just want to play football." It's very difficult because they have become used to that Premier League contract.'

I've always been amazed that more players don't use the PFA when it comes to negotiating contracts with their clubs, and instead prefer to use an agent. The PFA know the wage structure in place because they do the pensions, and they will perform a contract service for a fraction of what an agent will charge. There have also been cases in recent years of players being hit by a tax bill for the money earned by an agent who had negotiated a contract for them some years before. So, for example, an agent may have received £500,000 for his part in negotiating a player's contract, and although the player may not even be aware of the fee the agent got, the tax authorities may say that effectively the agent was employed by the player, and therefore it is taxed as a benefit in kind on that £500,000 from the player. For some it can amount to hundreds of thousands of pounds. Educating players about the consequences of something like this is another thing the PFA will try to do.

'You have to educate a player and sit down with him,' Bobby explains. 'We meet the players each year, and then there are also PFA delegates at clubs. One of the Premier League delegates suggested that it might be a good idea for young Premier League players to have their money put in a trust fund until they are twenty-three or twenty-four. They could access it before then for things like buying a house, but it would mean that the money is safe and there for them. If you're an eighteen-year-old kid and you've got a Premier League contract, for a lot of them that might be a very good contract but it might also be the only Premier League contract they have in their lives. So if they had a trust they'd have that money to fall back on if they did do something other than football or they went down the leagues.

'It's very difficult if you've been playing in the Premier League earning £1 million a year, and then your career doesn't work out as you thought it would. You have to go and play for a team in the lower leagues, and it's a real lifestyle change. There are so many pitfalls for young players. They get advice from us, but there are numerous people out there who see players as a meal ticket, as a cash machine. I always say that we ask so much of our young players and they're in the spotlight now at twenty-one or twenty-two.'

The PFA have sixty permanent staff, forty-five of them in Manchester and fifteen in their London office, and they also employ other staff on a part-time basis. They have departments for education, pensions, accident and medical insurance, counselling, coaching, and community and delegate liaison, and they also have people who will go to football clubs in order to deal with any problems from players. Footballers who come to this country from abroad and join the PFA are often amazed at the kind of services available to them, as well as at the difference from their home country with regard to getting paid.

'For example,' says Bobby, 'in the German Bundesliga, if say you're out injured for three months you don't get paid by the club. So unless you have an insurance policy in place you don't get any money. There are top clubs in Spain where players might not get their full wages because there's a law there that says if the club's losing money they can actually reduce the salaries of the players. We've got a football creditors rule in this country that means that every player is protected even if a club are in trouble. When that happens – and a club are struggling to pay the wages – we're usually the last resort. The club will come to us on the basis that no one else will give them money. Our aim then is to keep the club afloat as best we can, make loans to the club, and make sure the players and the staff get paid. More importantly, we get the players together and try to keep them together at the club. What you don't want is to have squads breaking up and players going off.

'There have been some success stories over the years with clubs who've been in administration and who we've helped. Clubs like Middlesbrough, Bolton and Swansea. In 2013 Swansea played Bradford in the League Cup Final, and both of these clubs were ones we'd helped to stay afloat. One of our biggest success stories was probably Portsmouth. One of our guys practically lived there for two years, and he would go in and deal with the players. We've been known to take along bags of money to hand out to players to make sure they get paid. There was one club we looked after, and their secretary used to hide the money from the chairman so that the players could get paid!'

Giving advice to players is obviously a big part of what the PFA are about. They are there twenty-four hours a day, and there is a helpline for their members if they need to call it. But whatever advice is given to a player, it's ultimately up to him to take it on board – and in the modern game there can be all sorts of things that might cause problems, from practical issues like fines from their clubs to the use of social media and what is acceptable 'banter' in the dressing room.

'All players need the PFA,' says Bobby. 'For example, players can only get fined two weeks' wages. There are clubs who would love to fine players three or four weeks' money, and clubs who'd like to sack them, but they can't do that because we've got things agreed as to what the fines are and what the sanctions are. A player can get a six-week fine, but that would be under exceptional circumstances. We go around every club and put on workshops where we sit down with players and are quite graphic about the sort of words they can and can't use in the dressing room. We say exactly what is and isn't acceptable, and tell them that they could end up with a five- or ten-match ban if they cross the line. We're trying to protect the players, and some of them need educating in the sense that they don't realise the implications of what they might say. Social media can also be a killer, and we've spoken to the boys about it. But the trouble is that some of them think they are a step ahead of the game or that they are just speaking to their mates. They don't realise that from the moment they put something out there it stays there.'

In the 1990s we went through a particularly difficult period at Charlton when some of our players tested positive for drug use. We naturally wanted to nip it in the bud, and in the end we adopted a zero-tolerance approach that saw us having to sack one of our most promising youngsters. When the whole situation occurred my first call was to the PFA to explain what was going on. I knew they'd get it – not just as PFA representatives but also as ex-players. Part of my thinking was also that I knew that by talking to them they in turn would talk to the player – and it would be a sensible conversation. I saw them as a body that could help me and help the situation I had on my hands.

'Most managers are former players anyway,' says Bobby. 'We want to protect our former players as well. With drugs, not only is it a sackable offence – it can potentially be a civil case as well, where a club might go after the player for a transfer fee. It's not just a case of a player losing his job and losing his income. He could end up bankrupt as well. That's why we're so strong on our education in terms of doping. Players have to be ultra-careful. These days players are front-page, back-page and gossip-page news. We try to protect players. If they do something wrong we don't condone what they've done, but we're a union and we're there to pick up the pieces and protect. Most of our staff are former players, and the reason for that is they know the dressing room – they know the industry.

'I've been with the PFA for seventeen years. Nothing really surprises me, and pretty much nothing fazes us as an organisation. When something happens it's a question of, "Oh, right. We'll deal with that." I've got the best job in the world – when you get up on a Monday morning and you don't know what's coming, but more importantly you're not frightened of what's coming.'

ONE OF THE bodies Bobby and the PFA have 'very cordial relations with' is the League Managers Association, or LMA. I have to declare an interest and say that I am on the board of the LMA, and have therefore seen up close what the organisation does. Its chief executive is Richard Bevan, who came to the organisation in 2008 after spending twelve years with the Professional Cricketers' Association, the last seven of those as their chief executive. During the time Richard has been at the LMA he has managed to move the organisation on in all sorts of directions. It is now a much more professional, business-like, forward-thinking organisation, with provocative plans for the future that will not only benefit its members but also football in this country. He clearly loves his job and the prospect of leading the LMA on to bigger and better things.

'I have worked for twenty-plus years in sporting associations, and I find the LMA the most interesting and challenging. It's also more like a family than any other,' he says. 'I have never seen anybody do their job with so much passion and dedication as a football manager, with so much resilience and often a lack of attention to their own health. I see the LMA as a very caring organisation and a very practical one. I like to think we are very professional in all aspects.

We're helping to take the collective voice of the managers and coaches to improve the game both on and off the pitch. We try to keep things very simple, and my job is really to be a facilitator. When our members have a problem we are there 24/7 – we find the very best professional to help. It might be a lawyer to assist with an employment situation, or a doctor, mentor, media trainer or career-guidance officer.

'We have an immensely talented team of sixteen people at the LMA, supported by an amazing network of people in sport and business that help the members when needed. Most of the people supporting our members are not actually from within football. We've grown the business tenfold from a turnover of £300,000 in recent years. The major supporter of the LMA is the Premier League, followed by the FA and the PFA, together with the two-thirds of our revenue coming from business. We have a very good business club, with forty business partners. If we generated another £1 million we would deliver more of the same in benefits, helping to identify players who want to be coaches, coaches who want to be managers, and assisting coaches and managers to survive long enough to build a career. We have 380 members – ninety-plus managers and coaches working in over thirty countries. There are also 650 coaches working who need greater support, and we help as much as we can.'

One of the things that Richard introduced to the LMA was a helpline for its members. The public might perhaps not realise it, but managers often find themselves in a very lonely place. Even the most experienced and successful managers will tell you that. Managers in the Premier League are well paid for what they do, but I once read an article in which a club chairman said he found it strange that one of his managers had found it a lonely job considering he was being paid about £3 million a year. The real point, however, is that money has nothing to do with it.

Of course, being financially secure helps anyone, but in terms of what the job entails, that loneliness can be felt just as acutely by a Premier League manager as it can by another manager operating on a shoestring in League Two. And it's not just the loneliness of the job that might be a problem. Managers can have all sorts of issues that they have to deal with, and introducing a confidential helpline has meant they are able to pick up a phone, talk to someone and get the help they need. Quite frankly, when it was introduced, I was a little shocked at how many people were using it.

'The helpline has developed with a number of outside mentors and advisors – in excess of twenty people – who are specialists in their field,' reveals Richard. 'The confidentiality aspect is absolutely vital in this public business of football. No board member – not even the chairman Howard Wilkinson – knows who has called the helpline. And it can be for all sorts of reasons. I had one very senior manager who rang me up to say that he just wanted to let me know that the support was amazing. He told me he'd had a player whose father had died and he didn't know how best to support the player. So he phoned the helpline and was getting advice on how to help him every day.'

The helpline is just one of the support mechanisms that are in place for all members of the LMA. Quite often the public will only hear about the LMA when there is a high-profile managerial sacking. Richard and his team do a fantastic job when this happens, but the services and resources they will offer to one of the game's big names are exactly the same as to any member in whatever division they are operating. The 'life expectancy' at any club for a Premier League manager averages now something like fifteen to sixteen months, and in the Championship it's less than a year. So when a manager does lose his job, what is the usual scenario for the LMA and what is the time of year they most dread?

'We take it in turns not to have Christmas. I remember once, from the Boxing Day into the first ten days of the New Year, we lost nine managers,' he says. 'Our team are there to listen and to offer support for the manager – and indeed his family. Often when a manager is sacked we know there may be a termination of contracts that's about to happen. There are a number of managers at any one time being advised on how to manage upwards and deal with the concerns of constructive dismissal. The manager will call to confirm he's been sacked – on too many occasions managers have been sacked on the phone. We then contact the club and help to ensure a professional process takes place. That is not as easy as it sounds, as the club are often slow putting details in writing. We agree the compensation deal as quickly as possible with the club, and where appropriate put a press release out for the manager.'

What Richard has described is a relatively straightforward case, where things are settled in a sensible way and there is no conflict between the manager and the club with regard to suitable compensation. But there are other cases where the legal setup he has introduced really comes into its own. I resigned from West Ham in 2008 because the clause I had in my contract saying that I would have final say on the selection of players to be transferred to and from the club was ignored when a player was sold. I brought a claim for wrongful dismissal and won the case. The QC I employed for the case was Paul Gilroy, and he did a very good job for me. Now that same Paul Gilroy is part of the LMA legal team, which is available to all of its members should they ever require it.

'When I joined the LMA the legal side of things was not quite as extensive as we needed,' says Richard. 'We now have two QCs – most people are unaware that you can instruct QCs directly. We also have in-house and top legal experts we use, depending on what the problem is. In 2014–15 there were 211 compromise agreements for managers and coaches, as 40 per cent of managers now don't get past seventy-five games and more than 50 per cent of first-time managers don't get a second opportunity. In many professions people will set a number of goals during their working lives. In football management many will say that the definition of success is survival! When it comes to the skills to be able to do the job, you need to be a leader, a manager and a coach. You need a really good eye for recruitment, you need to be an instinctive decision-maker, and you have to be resilient and be an excellent communicator.

'I think younger managers have realised very quickly that when you go into a club you're unlikely to be there as long as you might want. So really focusing on building your skill-set is a key goal, as is striving to reach 300 games as a manager and building a career from there.'

Education is now a big part of what the LMA is about. When you are looking to become a manager and you are offered a job, you can't say no because you're aware it might not happen again. In recent years I've found more and more from talking to young managers and coaches that they need experience – because you can't do the job without it. I think the LMA is very big on this fact, and they're saying, 'Look, when you get your first job, you've invariably got to be successful.' So I think that gaining as much experience and education before they get that job is essential. It wasn't really like that when I started in management twenty-five years ago. But now people who want to be managers and coaches are able to go on all sorts of courses and get qualifications like the LMA diploma in football management, or attend LMA masterclasses that cover a whole range of topics.

'The game should be identifying a player who wants to become a coach four or five years before he finishes playing,' insists Richard. 'During that period he should be looking to gain qualifications and some experience. He might start working in the academy, going on different courses, having access to mentors, attending masterclasses and then on to the pro licence. The FA delivers the licence courses, and we deliver very focused programmes. I spoke to a young coach recently who'd been on most of the masterclasses and had then found a job. He told me that he thought the difference between the pro licence and the masterclasses was that the masterclasses were very practical and focus on how best to survive long enough to win sufficient matches to build a career.

'Now we're finding that more of our members are asking to be supported on a one-to-one basis. Once we have raised new funds we will be rapidly expanding this area of support – how to manage upwards or even learning a new language, as many of our managers are now looking at working abroad.

'I asked a number of our business partners how much they spent on the development and training of their personnel. It was often 1 per cent of turnover – that might be in the many millions of pounds. In the world of football – up until two years ago – the amount of money spent on leadership and management training was close to zero. When it comes to having time for training, managers have something that many people in executive positions don't get – time off between jobs.'

Richard is clearly keen to keep moving on and explore new avenues that could be of benefit to the LMA membership. It's not just a case of a manager being in work, then getting sacked and waiting around for the next job that might come his way. It's a very competitive industry, with dozens of managers vying for one job when it becomes available. But the fact that there could be other roles for an experienced manager to fill is not lost on Richard.

'I had a call some time ago from a club and they asked me, "Can you advise us if there are managers who would be interested in a caretaker manager's role?" They said that they'd sacked their manager, didn't want to rush into an appointment and were looking for a caretaker. We can never offer advice that will prefer one member over another, but support with such things as CVs.

'Another vital support area is well-being and health care. One of the best things we offer our members is a fit to perform testing and free life scan test, which is basically a series of scans and tests of the blood and internal organs. Health care is so very important – not just the physical side but also the mental, such as coping with the stress of the job. Standing on the touchline, when the heart rate goes up from a standing start you can get large surges of adrenalin, which most men in their forties or fifties don't get, and which can cause issues. As a mature and responsible association we're in contact with all our members about a whole host of health and well-being matters.'

Whatever some people may think, managing a football club is not easy and you are learning all the time when you're in the job. There are a lot of pressures that go with it, and what you do as a job is also on show all the time. Some years ago when my son was still at school he came home quite upset one day because one of the other dads had made some comment about me possibly getting the sack. I went to collect my son from school the next day and made a point of talking to this particular dad. I asked him what he did for a living, and he told me he was a plumber. I told him in a jokey way that if he ever fitted a central-heating system and it didn't work properly he might not get paid for the job – but nobody would really hear about it. I was trying to make the point that whatever I did in my job was public knowledge. So if there was a mistake on a Saturday or my team didn't get the result they wanted it was all over the media, not just for one day, but for two or three. I wasn't asking for sympathy. I just wanted to explain how different it was for me and my family.

Nobody forced me to become a manager. I was given the opportunity and grabbed it with both hands. It's an addictive profession, but it can take its toll. There's really only a small group of people who know what it's like – your fellow managers – which is precisely why an association like the LMA is so important to the game.

CHAPTER 17

OWNER

David Sullivan

IT USED TO be something that was quite common in football. A supporter would do well in business, make a bit of money and then buy his local football club. These days, certainly in the top flight, that sort of thing doesn't really happen. For a start, fewer than half of the clubs in the Premier League are British-owned. And then when you look at the owners who *are* actually supporters of their clubs as well, that number reduces further.

Someone who has achieved his dream of owning the club he supported as a kid is David Sullivan, who, along with David Gold, bought West Ham United in 2010. Both men were childhood West Ham supporters, with Gold actually playing for the club as a youngster. The pair are joint chairmen, with David Sullivan owning a controlling stake in the club. Before taking over at West Ham they were owners of

Birmingham City for seventeen years, and in all Sullivan has more than twenty-three years' experience as a football club owner.

He was born in Wales and as a kid not only watched Newport but also Cardiff City, making his way to the ground as a seven-year-old with his mates from the council estate they all lived on at the time. When he was twelve his family moved to Hornchurch in Essex and that was when he became a West Ham fan, watching them whenever he could. Although it would be quite a few years before he'd actually own a football club, it was a role he began thinking about long before he had the money to invest in Birmingham in 1993, as he explains.

'When I was a kid I had a fantasy that I'd buy Newport County, who were the team I used to go and watch at the time. I dreamed of buying them, and then buying the whole Welsh team so that overnight they'd become a really good side. The Welsh team were pretty good back in the late 1950s and reached the World Cup Finals in Sweden. So I had this fantasy of being the owner of a football club, and it went way back to when I was a kid. Life's about chasing your dreams, and by the time I was twenty-seven I was already a millionaire a few times over. Nine years later I'd made even more money, and that was when I started to think about owning a football club. I looked at buying Watford, I looked at Leeds and I looked at Bradford. People knew I was looking to buy a club, and I was shown something in the *Financial Times* saying that the people who owned Birmingham City were in administration. They had an administrator who was selling the club, so I bought Birmingham – and that was the start of it.

'I'm good with stats, and I remembered that a few years earlier Birmingham had played in front of about 30,000 people in what was Division One. I thought any club who can get that sort of crowd in that division were worth getting involved with. With all due respect to some clubs, you can't build them up because the support just isn't there. But I thought that Birmingham were potentially a big club – they were in a big city and they had decent support. I suppose it was really a rich man chasing his dream, his fantasy, but we knew we could build something bigger. We stayed for seventeen years, and in those last nine years that we were there we were either in the Premier League or promoted to the Premier League.

'We left a good team when we left Birmingham, but at the end it was like a marriage that had gone sour and you wanted out. Although we left them with a good team, eighteen months earlier the fans were tearing down the goalposts – there was a lot of abuse from them. One of my kids was traumatised by the abuse, and that's when I started to think, "I've got to get out of here." We were always outsiders, the cockneys in Birmingham. They really want their own, and if anyone said to me, "Should I buy a football club?" I'd say, "If you buy your local club it's a tremendous feeling."

That, in effect, was what David Sullivan and David Gold did when they bought West Ham in 2010. The boys who had 'done good' bought the team they supported. They were not only owners, they were fans as well.

'We're genuine supporters,' insists Sullivan. 'When we lose we're down on the ground as supporters and we're down on the ground as financial investors. Our hurt is double! It ruins our weekend, and it hurts most when we lose to a team that we think we should have beaten – it's bloody horrible! The other season, when the team had underperformed in some of the away games and they had a plane taking them back, you feel like saying, "You can have the coach back tonight!"

'I think the fans accept that you're trying to do your best for the club. You don't always get it right, but I think as long as they see you're trying they're okay. It's amazing how many successful businessmen can't make football clubs work. The point is, football's like no other business. You can't project your income very accurately because it depends on how you perform on the pitch. However well you run the business you are dependent on what happens on a Saturday, and you get injuries.

'I think you've got to show a bit of ambition for the supporters. You can't just run it as a business to make a profit or break even. As I see it, you're building a brand, you're building a club. We inherited £100 million of debt when we bought the club, and one day I want the club to be financially self-sufficient. But I've got to do it slowly. It's a balancing act, but as I say, you're trying to do your best for the club.

'When you first come into a club as the owner and you've never been in that position before, it takes you about a year or eighteen months before you really start to understand the football world. At Birmingham when we first took over we didn't have a clue about anything. We were facing relegation and the manager Terry Cooper said that if he got four players at £250,000 each he'd keep us up and we'd do a lot better the following season. We stayed up on the last day of that season, and the celebrations were like we'd won the World Cup.

'The next season Terry left in the November and Barry Fry came in as manager. He said, "I'll get you out of the division," which he did, but we went down not up – although we did come up the season after that. We signed Ricky Otto, who was a winger, for £800,000, which was a lot of money for us, and Barry said, "Oh, I've made a mistake, I need a centre-forward!" So we then went and signed Kevin Francis from Stockport.

'Barry got us back up in the Championship and we stayed up, but we didn't do that well and we got rid of Barry. It's one of my deep regrets, because if we were the people we are now we wouldn't have got rid of Barry – I'd have given him at least another year and signed some more players with him. We were just naïve, but we're still very friendly with him now. What happens when you're new to everything is that people influence you. They say, "You should be doing this" or "You should be doing that." Your head is spinning. What I would say about football is that nobody knows all the answers, particularly when it comes to signings.

'At Birmingham we were quite frugal, and in the last nine years we were there we didn't have to put any money in. At West Ham I see it as more of a long-term thing. Without going bust, I realise that we've got to make substantial signings every year to keep the supporters happy and, as a supporter myself, to sell the dream. But whenever you sign someone there's an element of risk. If you sign someone from abroad there's a bigger risk – if you sign someone from England there's less risk, but it's more expensive.'

Making signings each season and the type of signings that a club make are crucial if a team is going to grow and improve. David seems to be very much a hands-on owner, and he is the one who does most of the deals the club are involved in when it comes to player recruitment. Any owner or chairman has to have a good relationship with their manager, which means being able to trust their judgement when it comes to playing matters and players.

'What happens with a manager is that initially you back him 100 per cent because you believe in his judgement. But as time goes on you start to question his judgement when you've had a few dud buys,' he says with a smile. 'I've always said to a manager at the start, "Look, you will pick 80 per cent of the players and I will support you. One out of ten I'll block you because I can't live with the player, and one out of ten I'm going to give you a player you may not fancy. I'm going to say, 'I fancy him – and if it goes wrong, blame me.'"

'It was like the thing that happened with Diafra Sakho in the summer of 2014. Sam Allardyce was our manager and wanted to buy Connor Wickham. I wanted Sakho and he reluctantly agreed to take Sakho. We flew him over and did his medical, and then Sam says to me that he's changed his mind. So I said, "Okay, Sam, it's your call. But I'm not happy." We sent the kid back, and he was in tears – it was his big chance. I asked Sam who he wanted instead. He said Connor Wickham, and that he'd been told Sunderland would take £5 million for him. So I phoned Sunderland up, and they said he's not for sale. I said, "Will you take £5 million?" They said no. I said, "Will you take £7 million?" They said no. So we had twenty-four hours to go before the deadline. I said let's take Sakho, which was what we did. So that's how that one happened. But in the main the manager says he wants a player – and you go and get him.

'Sometimes there'll be players that you take a chance with and hope they come off, but you're always looking for an exit. If it goes wrong, how can I get out of the deal? You're paying £3 million, £4 million or £5 million for a player. You want them on five-year contracts, or four-year contracts with a two-year option so that they don't walk out on you. At the same time you don't want to be stuck with them if it doesn't work out, so you're thinking if the wages are manageable there's an exit route. In the main, you can only sign players the manager wants, and I like a manager to be a manager.

'We have a certain amount for transfers, and at the start of the 2015–16 season we decided to go for three or four players that were better than what we had, rather than go for numbers. We wanted to try and look for a bit of quality. What you have to do in the window is to get some players in and then get some out. You might then be in a position to go again and buy more players right at the death because there might be some bargains, but you can't rely on doing your business then. At the start of the season you might have already played five or six games, so that's 15 per cent of the season gone. I know fans don't want to hear it, but once you've spent your money it's gone. You can't dig it up again. That money's gone.

'Transfers are complicated and they can take a lot of time to get across the line. Agents want more and more, particularly with the TV money going up. They're getting very greedy. I do most of the deals, and often you will get an agent saying, "I can get you this player for this amount," and you're suckered in. Then they can't get him for what they said and the fee goes up. It's so wearing. You're trying to do your best for the club, and perhaps the most difficult thing is trying to get a clause into a player's contract that says if the club are relegated the player's salary is halved. Which actually is still not enough, because if you're relegated your income as a club goes down by way more than half. But if your wages come down by half, it's a contribution. Where that sort of thing goes out of the window is when you get a top player who says, "I'm not signing that. If you go down, that's your problem."

'Now some clubs won't sign a player unless they sign that clause. We've signed a few who have, but if you're Manchester United they'll sign it, and they'll sign it if you're Tottenham, Arsenal, Chelsea, Manchester City or Liverpool, because it would have to be a very freak year for any of them to be relegated. I've got players to sign it, but sometimes you have to say, "If we're relegated your salary will be halved, but you can leave for a nominal fee or a reduced fee."

'When it comes to loans for a season you can only loan two from England, but you can loan as many as you like from abroad. It's a nonsense, really. If they want to help young English players they should definitely change the rules, so that if there are players under twenty-one or twenty-two years of age they don't count as an English loan. If you really want to help young English players and let them play in the Premier League they shouldn't let them count as part of the two-loan thing. Then the lesser Premier League clubs would loan the players – and it would give those players a chance.'

One of the other things that David has had to do over the years, both at Birmingham and at West Ham, is to hire and fire managers. Both he and David Gold have been supportive of their managers, but there comes a time when an owner, for whatever reason, believes it is time for a change. Most often these days it is because of a bad run of form, where the results have gone wrong and the team is losing. It might be a cliché, but when people talk about football being a results business it has never been more the case than it is in the modern game. As a manager you ideally want the backing of the owner – and the time to build the team and the club. But the reality these days is that it doesn't happen. This is particularly the case in the Premier League, where the rewards are so great. Nobody wants to lose their Premier League status, and after a run of six or eight bad results clubs will often press the panic button, with an owner looking for another manager who they think can rescue the situation.

During his time at West Ham David Sullivan has had to make some crucial managerial decisions. When he and David Gold arrived at the club Gianfranco Zola was the manager, but he was soon replaced by Avram Grant, who lasted for just one season as the Hammers found themselves relegated from the Premier League. In 2011 West Ham appointed Sam Allardyce as their manager on a four-year deal, and he had a pretty clear remit – to get the club promoted and then to make sure they stayed in the Premier League. He did both, gaining promotion via the play-offs in his first season and then finishing tenth, thirteenth and twelfth in the Premier League. But his contract was not renewed, and in the summer of 2015 West Ham appointed one of their former players, Slaven Bilic, as manager at the start of their last season at Upton Park before moving into the Olympic Stadium at Stratford.

Making the right choice as manager is always important for an owner, and to do so they have to look at what they want that manager to be, and what they want him do in the short and long term. They also have to decide how they want him to play – are they looking for a defensive or an attacking manager? – and whether they are prepared to take a gamble on a young, inexperienced manager or would prefer a vastly experienced one, possibly with European or international experience. It's a lot to consider, and, with the move to the Olympic Stadium imminent, David Sullivan knew that getting what he considered to be the right man would be absolutely central to the club's move and their progression beyond that.

'It's very hard picking a manager,' he admits. 'As an owner you probably pick a manager every three or four years. When it came to replacing Sam we were looking for someone with a proven record who was experienced – and we aimed high. When we appointed Sam we wanted him to get us promotion, which he did, and then keep us up and establish us in the Premier League. At the end it was very difficult because we had a situation where we'd won three out of twenty-one matches, and you combine that with the fact that the manager was tired and wanted a break – and he was unpopular with the supporters, which doesn't help. I know that's not the be-all and end-all – but if he'd stayed and at the start of the season we'd had a couple of bad results, they could have turned on him and the team. So you have to find another manager. And it's difficult.

'After Sam we aimed very high. We spoke to Rafa Benítez, and he was within two hours of signing for us. He wanted to come back to England but he was delaying and delaying, and then out of the blue Real Madrid came in for him. The Italian team manager showed a little bit of interest, and the Sevilla manager was another one. We spoke to Jürgen Klopp. He didn't say no, but said he wanted a couple of weeks to think about it. I'd spoken to Slaven some years before about coming to the club, and it never happened. But this time we decided to go with him.'

Moving to a new stadium will give West Ham increased capacity, and the club will be able to exploit all the commercial opportunities that go with having the new ground. Staying in the Premier League is of paramount importance, but so is growing the club. Being the owner of his local club means something to David Sullivan, and I think it means something to the fans as well. He's seen a lot of change in the game since he and David Gold took their first steps as owners with Birmingham City, and much of it has been for the good. But there is one thing that saddens him – the lack of contact with many of the foreign owners.

'It's one of my deepest regrets these days,' he says. 'Even when a foreign owner is at a game, they go into their box and don't say hello. Roman Abramovic did come to a game when we were at Birmingham and I met him. He also came into the boardroom at West Ham, but he doesn't go into the Chelsea boardroom. Even when there are Premier League meetings the foreign owners will just send their executives, so you're not actually meeting your counterparts. It's one area where football has gone backwards. You're not meeting other owners.'

ACKNOWLEDGEMENTS

I WOULD LIKE to thank all the people who gave up their precious time to talk to me and contribute to this book with frankness and honesty, to Phil Smith at First Artist, to Tom Whiting, and to Jack Fogg and everyone at HarperCollins for their help and encouragement in wanting to produce something for the football fan that is hopefully not only interesting, but different from many other books about the game. Finally, I would like to thank writer Kevin Brennan for his patience and help in putting everything together.